Praise for Sell•er•ship

"Sell-er-ship is the new buzz word for making a positive impact within any organization."
–Jeffrey Hayzlett, Founder C-suite Network

"Finally! A book that effectively (and creatively) walks salespeople through the process of growing into leadership. Whether you are in sales or already in management leading a team, Sellership is a must read!"
–DeAnne Stidham, President and Co-Founder of LuLaRoe

"The ideal story for anyone going into the sales industry."
–Stephen Van Deventer, Founder, Preveceutical

"A must read for anyone transitioning from selling to leading."
–Dan McCormick, Host of the Greatest Salesman Podcast, Ambassador, Og Mandino Company

Sell·er·ship

(n.) How top salespeople become remarkable sales leaders

A leadership parable by:

Ben Ward & Dr. Greg Reid

Sell•er•ship

How Top Salespeople Become Remarkable Sales Leaders

Copyright © 2021

ISBN: 978-1-7351657-3-8

Joint Venture Publishing

Blue Sky R&D, LLC

Printed in the United States of America

Dedication

This book is dedicated to Doug Johnson, a highly influential leader in my life.

I always knew that Doug believed in me, and because of this, in his presence, I became the best version of myself. My life changed forever when I overheard him privately telling another person, "That Ben Ward, I would invest in stock in him." When he showed up to my baseball games, I played better. When he challenged me to step up at times, I knew it was because he had my best interest at heart. He inspired me to stretch my limits. Doug is a true leader and an incredible example of the principles in this book.

Thank you, Doug. I love you, brother!

Acknowledgements

This book would not have been possible without the contributions of many.

Thank you to Team Sellership, you helped me make this book a reality and something I am proud of;

My book partner, Greg Reid, is an incredible human being and has the energy of a small army. His expert guidance and creativity on this project have been absolutely profound. Greg's passion for living and serving others lights a fire in any room he enters, and he is a powerful leader;

And Patti McKenna, who helped give meaning to the ideas and concepts in the book and is the kindest and most effective person to work with—thank you;

To my wife, Sheri, who has sacrificed everything and stuck by me throughout the years as I have worked and learned the principles in this book. I could not have done this without her;

To our children, Miley, McKay, and Emery, you inspire me every day and bring the sweetest joy into my life. As your dad, I am humbled and grateful to pass the principles in this book on to you.

I am also grateful to those who had a direct impact on this book, before, during, and after the writing process. My special thanks to: The team at Joint Venture Publishing; Shannon Parsons, for all her help in making this book a reality; Wright Thurston, who has been a highly impactful mentor, leader, and partner while I led sales teams in the trenches over the past 20 years; Jared Taggart, my first sales manager who taught me so much about what it takes to be a successful leader; Kenny and Jill Brady. Kenny, who bleeds the principles in this book, and I have enjoyed hundreds of hours of discussion around them, and we have traveled all over America together teaching many of them. And to Jill for using her wordsmith skills to make this book read even better; Josh Steimle and Jess Larsen with the crew at Published Author's Mastermind who helped every step of the way to bring this book to life; and Brian Tracy, for his profound influence in planting the seed for this book in a conversation years ago with me and for generously writing the foreword.

It would be impossible for me to mention everyone who helped shape me and this book, although I trust that you know who you are. I thank you all for your contribution in making this book a success.

Ben Ward

Table of Contents

Author's Note

Throughout my career in sales, leading sales teams, and mentoring sales leaders, I've uncovered an often overlooked truth: selling and leading require different skillsets. Perhaps that sounds obvious, and maybe the difference doesn't seem to be all that drastic on the surface.

Yet, over and over again, I see successful salespeople promoted to positions of leadership because, well, logic would suggest that a person performing well in one task is well suited to lead others in performing that same task. However, they aren't the same tasks at all, are they? Selling is not the same as leading. This isn't to say however, that successful salespeople can't become effective leaders. In fact, with the right guidance, they can become *great* leaders. And herein lies an opportunity for the sales industry.

Introducing Sellership!

Through over 20 years as a leader in the trenches, mentoring tens of thousands of sales leaders, I've developed a seven-step framework that helps transform high-performing salespeople into remarkable leaders.

I've learned that there's a set of common ingredients that help people who are great at sales transition into becoming successful leaders. I have embedded these principles into the story in this book.

Leaders who successfully make the shift from selling to effective leading are able to enjoy the following results:

- 10X team sales results without having to manipulate or babysit

- Become highly respected as a leader

- Create lasting impact and influence

- Increased personal and professional fulfillment

- Achieve meaningful connections across a wide variety of personalities

- Duplicate and multiply success

- Create leveraged results through the efforts of others

I hope you enjoy reading *Sellership.* Above all, I hope that this story introduces the principles that will help you lead your sales teams to success.

SCAN ME

Enjoy this FREE resource guide! We invite you to scan, download, and save it to your desktop or print this guide to help retain and apply the principles of Sellership.

Foreword

For decades, I have been dedicated to accelerating success in sales and leadership. Throughout the years, I have identified the qualities that make great salespeople and highly impactful sales leaders. However, I have learned that the characteristics of a successful salesperson aren't necessarily the qualities that are needed to be an effective leader.

The most impactful leaders are committed to continuous learning and growing and know how to unlock the best within those they lead. Ben Ward understands these qualities and what it takes to succeed at a high level in both sales and in leadership. Many of the principles taught in this book are original, having been borne out of his personal experience in successfully leading sales teams over the years.

The characters in this book will take you on a multi-tiered journey of growth. You will meet Matt, an aspiring young salesperson, and his mentor, Rae, who has recently been promoted to a leadership role under the guidance of their division president, Dan. Their challenges reveal success principles unique to their position—principles that every leader can use to increase their knowledge and value in business, as well as in life.

If you lead a sales team, I'm confident you will find this a valuable and enjoyable read.

Brian Tracy
BrianTracy.com

(1) Transition to Leading

Standing in the bank lobby, Matt inserted his debit card in the ATM and punched in his four-digit PIN. When his transaction options popped onto the screen, Matt held his breath. He knew he had to check his balance, but he was afraid to punch the button and actually see just how bad it was. Taking a deep breath, he bit the bullet and checked his balance. A feeling of dread overcame him when he saw that he only had $18.50 in available funds. Sighing, he realized that he didn't have enough money in his account to withdraw any funds—the minimum withdrawal at the ATM was $20. Grabbing the receipt that reflected his meager balance, he stared at it, as if confirming that there was no mistake. But he knew it wasn't a mistake. With a deep sigh, he accepted the reality that he was down to his last few dollars. For now, he'd have to get by with the cash in his pocket, which wasn't much.

I don't know what I'm going to do, he thought, *but I need to get my head straight and I need to do it now!*

Consumed with worry, he walked the block to the bagel shop, realizing his bank account mirrored what his girlfriend, Tessa, had said just the week before. Giving back the cubic zirconia engagement ring he'd given her three months earlier, she said, "Matt, I love you, but there's no way we're going to be able to get married. You can't afford a wife and family. You can't even afford to take care of yourself." He'd played those words in his mind a thousand times, and while he knew they were harsh, in his heart, he also knew they were true.

Pushing the front door open, he was so preoccupied that he didn't notice anyone was behind him ... until the door abruptly stopped as it swung shut. Startled, he looked back to see that he had nearly let it slam on a woman who had obviously been just a step or two behind him. Quickly trying to recover, he grabbed the door and attempted to apologize.

"I'm so sorry. I didn't see you there. I guess I was lost in thought ... but that's no excuse," he rambled.

"That's okay, don't worry about it," she replied.

Embarrassed, Matt approached the counter, where he ordered his usual: a plain white bagel with strawberry cream cheese. The man who took his order asked, "Would you like anything else with that?"

"Thanks, a cold-pressed juice sounds good," Matt answered as he looked down at his money clip.

"Okay, a bagel with strawberry cream cheese and a medium cold-pressed juice. That'll be $10.25," the man smiled.

Hearing the total, Matt quickly changed his mind. "Thanks, but I think I'll just have the bagel today, and maybe a cup of water."

Standing behind him, the woman observed the interaction. Initially, she had been taken aback, thinking that Matt was just another inconsiderate kid who hadn't been taught that it was common courtesy to hold a door open when someone was behind him. But as she watched and listened, she could tell there was more going on. She sympathized with him as he changed his order. The young man seemed anxious, and at the same time, like his thoughts were elsewhere.

He's obviously going through something, she thought. *But he still took the time to apologize to me.* She realized that she'd been lost in thought, coming up with a story and explanation about someone she had never met before and knew nothing about. She shook her head as if to snap out of it.

"That'll be five dollars," the clerk smiled as he handed him his bagel and water.

Matt slowly peeled a $10 bill from his money clip and handed it over. Anxiously, he waited for his change, and then double checked to make sure it was all there before he pocketed it.

Placing the five-dollar bill next to the four ones in his clip, he let out a sigh. *I better make it last,* he thought.

"Thank you," he said to the clerk. As he walked away from the counter, he abruptly stopped and turned back to the woman who had been standing behind him. "Again, I'm sorry. I didn't mean to be rude."

It was obvious that his words were sincere and genuine, and the woman responded in kindness. "It's fine," she smiled. "Really. I don't want you to worry about it at all."

Nodding his head, he attempted a smile and walked out the door, this time, obviously looking to make sure no one was behind him.

The woman watched as he exited the building and walked across the glass windows.

Not ten feet from the door, Matt passed an older man sitting on the sidewalk. He held a tattered hat in his lap, waiting for passersby to drop in a handful of coins or an occasional dollar. Upon seeing the man, Matt's initial thought was that he was going to be in the same situation soon if he didn't find a job. But then he realized that wasn't the case. No matter what, he would still be more fortunate than this panhandler—he might be down to his last few dollars, but he knew he had to keep pushing forward.

For the second time in the last few minutes, Matt abruptly stopped and turned around. Approaching the man, he reached into his pocket for his money clip and pulled the $5 bill out. "Here you go. Don't spend it all in one place," he smiled, trying to interject some lightness to the man's situation—and his own.

"I can't guarantee that," the man laughed. "But thank you very much. You have a blessed day."

"I can't guarantee that, either," Matt responded with a halfhearted smile.

Standing in front of the bagel shop, half-eaten bagel in hand, the woman overheard the exchange. *Here is a young man who seems to have troubles of his own, yet he's still giving to someone less fortunate,* she thought.

This was the last piece she needed to be convinced that he was the type of person she was looking for to potentially join her team. Immediately, she picked up her pace to try to catch up to Matt as he walked to the other end of the block. As he neared the bus stop, she feared he would climb aboard, and she wouldn't have an opportunity.

"Wait!" she yelled. "Wait a minute! Stop!"

Turning his head to see what was going on, Matt immediately noticed the same woman from the bagel shop running toward him. Awkwardly, he stood there, wondering what she wanted … and if she was even talking to him.

"I'm sorry," she said, a bit out of breath. "I was afraid I wouldn't catch you."

"Is something wrong? Did I drop something?" Matt asked.

"Oh, no. Everything's fine. But I was hoping you might have a minute to talk with me," she said. "I didn't mean to intrude, but I couldn't help but notice your kind gesture back there when you went out of your way to help that old man. A lot of people would have just pretended he wasn't there."

"Well, I wish I could have given more, but …" Matt said, stopping just short of admitting just how bad his situation was.

"The point is, you did something, and that's what matters," she interjected. "Before we go any further, let me introduce myself. My name is Raela, but most people call me Rae."

"Hi, Rae. My name is Matt," he replied with a smile.

"Matt, after running into you, and watching you a bit this morning, I want to commend you. I can see that you genuinely care about people. You have an obvious sense of pride, but it's also obvious that you are a humble young man. I admire that."

Matt shuffled his feet, slightly embarrassed to receive a compliment from a complete stranger. "I appreciate your kind words," was the only response he could muster.

"Matt, I was wondering if you would consider coming to my office this afternoon—say, about 12:30 or so. My company has an opening, and we're looking for the right person to fill it. I can't promise you a job, but after meeting you today, I can definitely get you an interview. You seem to be just the type of person we like to see on our team. If you're free to stop by, I can fill you in," the woman said.

"A job opening? Uh, sure, I can be there," Matt responded in surprise.

"Great. Here's my business card. My office is on the third floor. Just tell the receptionist you're there to see me. I look forward to it," she smiled before she turned to walk back down the street.

What just happened? Matt asked himself as he thought about the turn of events. *Here I was nearly frantic about not having any money and out of the blue, someone approaches me about a job. That just doesn't happen.*

Matt walked off the elevator and into a large reception room, where he approached a young woman sitting behind a half circle desk.

"Hi, I'm Matt," he said. "I have an appointment to see Rae, uh Raela."

"You've got an appointment to see Rae? Good for you—things are about to go your way. Rae has a knack for making things happen," she said as she rose and led him to a corner office.

"Make yourself comfortable, Matt," Rae motioned toward a chair. "Let's sit over here at the table. I hope you don't mind, but I took the liberty of ordering us lunch from the new deli down the street I've been wanting to try."

"No, that's fine. I mean, that's very nice of you," he corrected himself.

As Matt filled himself up on a sandwich piled high with pastrami, he listened as Rae shared some information about her company. They were a solar, energy, and home automation company and specialized in residential and commercial sales. She explained that they had nine members on board and were looking for a tenth person to join their team and start training next week.

"So, what do you think?" she asked. "Are you interested in interviewing for the position?"

"Well, yes. But I have to confess, I don't have any sales experience, so I don't think I'm qualified," he answered.

"That may be even better. You won't already have any bad habits that we have to correct," she replied. "We do have to go through the formalities, though. I need you to complete an application, and you'll have to receive management approval. While I can't make any promises, I can put in a good word for you."

"I understand," he said, looking over the application she handed him. "I appreciate everything you've done already, really I do."

When their luncheon meeting was over, Matt left, with Rae's promise to contact him sometime within the next 48 hours. The first thing she did was look over his employment history. *Hmm, just as I thought. He's been unemployed for about six months now,* Rae thought to herself before she walked the application to talk through it with Dan, the division president, who she reported to.

"I know he has no experience, but I like him. He's a bright and personable young man, and I can sense that he's eager and has a desire to help others—all good qualities that would benefit our team," she said.

Dan took a few minutes to review the application before sharing his thoughts.

"You've always been a good judge of character, Rae, and if you think he has potential, you have my full support," he said.

Late that afternoon, Matt received a phone call from Rae.

"Hi, Matt. I was able to get you an interview, but there is a mandatory informational meeting you'll have to attend first. Can you be here Monday morning, 9 a.m. sharp?" she asked.

Matt readily agreed. When he hung up, he replayed the day through his head and thought about everything that had transpired. His thoughts turned to the man sitting on the sidewalk and the fact that Rae had witnessed him giving him a few dollars. At the time, it was all he really could give, but as his day unfolded and he received unexpected blessings, he couldn't help but think about how much he valued that five dollars when he gave it away … not to mention how hard it was to give it away. The truth was that it was even foolish in his situation. Feeling grateful, he realized how much more valuable that money would be if he could land this job. The irony was not lost on Matt; by giving that five dollars away, he just might be the one who benefited most of all.

(2) The Window and the Mirror

To Matt's surprise, the conference room was packed on Monday morning. He had no idea that there would be so many people vying for the position. When he saw that nearly every chair was taken, the high hopes he'd had all weekend plummeted. But he also knew that he didn't have any other opportunities knocking on his door, so he figured he'd stick it out, at least for the time being. He had to give it a chance—for himself, for Tessa, and for his bank account.

Shortly after he took a seat, Rae walked to the front of the room.

"Welcome, everyone. It's great to see such a good turnout this morning. Today, you're going to learn about our company and what we have to offer—to you and to our customers. Our sales representatives enjoy an incredible opportunity to set their own income and enjoy the benefits of being among the top in their field," Rae announced.

Matt listened as she described the opportunity. It was a door-to-door sales job, and she touted an excellent support staff. In addition to their personal efforts, the company would generate leads and set appointments for them. Although this was a challenging job, the commission structure would give them the potential to earn six figures in the very first year.

When she was done, she introduced several of their successful salespeople, who shared their testimonials. After hearing testimonials from other salespeople and watching a PowerPoint presentation that explained the company's mission and services, the group broke for lunch.

"I'll see you all back here in an hour," she said.

At 1:00 sharp, Matt walked back in the conference room, thinking he must have misunderstood the time. The once full room now held only about a dozen people. The rest of the chairs were noticeably empty.

"Welcome back." Rae no sooner got the words out of her mouth when the guy sitting to Matt's right raised his hand.

"Hey, I'm sorry, I'm really not that interested in the position. And I just got a phone call—I can't stick around," he said, as he rose and walked out of the room.

"Where did everybody else go?" Matt asked, looking around at the number of empty chairs.

"The Bermuda Bathroom," Rae replied.

"The what?"

"The Bermuda Bathroom. They all leave to go to the bathroom or wherever and don't come back. It happens all the time," she explained. "At least that guy came back and let us know he wasn't interested. Most don't."

"That's not right," he commented.

"It's the way this industry is. Door-to-door sales aren't for everybody. Chances are that our numbers will diminish even more. It actually helps us weed out those who are not a good fit."

She was right. At the end of the day, there were only a handful of them left in the room—and they were the applicants who would be considered for Rae's new sales team.

Rae took a few minutes to converse with the group, letting them know they could expect a call to schedule an interview in the next few days.

Matt's meeting was scheduled for Wednesday afternoon. Straightening the collar of his button-up shirt, the elevator climbed to the third floor, and he stepped out into what was now a familiar area—the third-floor reception area.

"Good morning," he said as he approached the desk and announced that he was there for an interview with Rae.

However, he didn't meet only with Rae. She was right—she got him the interview, but not the job. When he walked into the interview, he was introduced to Dan, the division president, and another sales representative by the name of Carrie. Matt was glad that they didn't spend too much time dwelling on his sales experience, or rather lack thereof, instead devoting many of their inquiries to vague questions. They asked about his five and ten-year goals and whether he'd ever been in a position where he experienced conflict or setbacks … and how he had handled it. They wanted to know his strengths, and they asked him to describe his motivators. They were all questions he hadn't been prepared for, and as a result, he was sure he had botched up the interview.

Throughout, he kept trying to read Rae's face, looking for a reaction, but there wasn't one. She remained as she had from the first time he'd seen her in the bagel shop, professional and friendly. Following her lead, he shook everyone's hands when the interview was completed and thanked them for the opportunity to discuss his qualifications. When he left, though, the last thing he expected was a job offer.

But that was what he got. The next day, Rae called him and told him that the interview committee all thought he would be a great addition to their team. After she presented the details of the offer and Matt accepted, his new leader told him to report for training the next Monday.

Matt was among four new employees in the sales training—all were faces he recognized, for they were the only ones who had stuck it out during the informational meeting. By the end of the week morning, though, that number had dwindled down, and Matt found that he was the only one left.

"Matt, there are a few things I want to cover this morning. I do have a sales call this afternoon, though. Somebody has to meet potential customers," she smiled. "Why don't you come along and get some training in real time?"

Excited at the prospect of actually being on a sales call, Matt readily agreed, thinking it would be a nice change of pace to the information-packed classroom atmosphere where he'd spent the week. Rae explained that they were meeting with a couple in their early 30's who were interested in automating their home and potentially converting to solar energy. As a solar, energy, and home automation company, this couple was an ideal client because their generation was, for the most part, "green." Their generation grew up aware of the environment and the footprint fossil fuels left behind. In addition, they were today's version of the Jetson's, a space-age cartoon that depicted how people in the future lived with fully-automated appliances, even robots. Technology and automation were the toys of this age group, and homeowners like them sought the most advanced products for home security, automation, and interconnectivity.

Matt sat quietly and listened as Rae explained their product offerings and demonstrated some of their features.

"I understand that you recently purchased your home," she said. "Solar energy is one of the best investments you can make. Not only will it increase the value of your home, but it will significantly decrease your utility costs. It is one improvement you can make that will bring you a real return on your investment," she explained.

"I don't know," the woman said. "It seems like a lot of money, more than we were looking to spend right away."

Then looking at her husband, she said, "Why don't we get some other estimates? I know we wanted to have this done before my parents come for the holidays, but maybe we shouldn't rush into anything just yet."

Until then, Matt had stood silently in the background, listening to Rae's sales pitch. However, when the woman made this remark, he jumped into the conversation, forgetting that he was still a student in training.

"Oh, you're having guests for the holidays? My parents always have a house full during the holidays. Everywhere you look there are blankets and pillows," he laughed. "But it's always a good time.

Actually, holidays wouldn't be the same without a house full of relatives."

"Yes. We bought this house in the spring. For the first time, we have a guest room and don't have to ask our parents to stay at a hotel when they visit," she said. "But I don't want the house to be under construction while they're here, so maybe we should wait."

Rae saw an opening and went for it.

"There's no need to worry about that. I can guarantee that your upgrades will be installed within the next two weeks, and I'll even throw in an automated climate control system for free. Your parents will be able to control the temperature of their room with a simple voice command. You won't have to have spare blankets on hand if it gets chilly or a fan if it's too warm. The room temperature will be consistent morning and night. You can rest assured knowing your parents really are comfortable. It's kind of like living in San Diego," she chuckled. "The technology is so easy to use and provides so many benefits that your parents are going to be impressed and proud of the investment you've made and the value you're adding to your new home."

Thirty minutes later, the paperwork was signed, and they were out the door and in Rae's car.

"Matt, do you see what I did there?" Rae asked.

"You made a sale?" the sales trainee answered, stating the obvious.

"Well, yes, but it's not what I did; it's how I did it. It's all about perceived value," she explained.

"What do you mean by perceived value?"

"I had already explained the cost of the system, right? But before I let that set in, I automatically increased the value in their minds by including an automated climate control system at no cost. Now, they're getting more for their dollar—and naturally, the value of our system went up in their mind. Then, I added in the other benefits—their parents would be comfortable no matter what—all it would take for them to provide them with the perfect place to stay was a simple voice command. But then I showed them how it would make them *feel*—it would give them peace of mind, their parents would be impressed and, most of all, proud. To them that was perhaps more valuable than the benefits of an energy-saving solar system and the value of upgrading their home to be energy efficient."

"Wow. I didn't think of it that way—but now that you point it out, I can see that it totally shifted the sale. I have to admit, for a few minutes there, I was pretty sure they had already made their minds up and you weren't going to get a sale," Matt said. "And I do want to apologize. I think I spoke out of turn. It wasn't my place to enter the conversation."

"It could have gone either way. Depending on what you said, of course. Thankfully, this time, no damage was done," she smiled. "Perhaps, we got lucky in that you said the right thing. Anyway, all's well that ends well. You just helped me discover their problem sooner."

"Well, I'm glad I didn't mess it up," Matt sighed.

"Matt, people don't buy products—they buy solutions," his leader and trainer advised.

"What was their problem?" Matt asked.

"As they've been thinking about getting solar energy, they really didn't *need* automated climate control. But they did want to make sure their parents were comfortable, and I was able to show them how we can make sure they will be," she smiled.

"That's cool," Matt said. "So what's next? What are we going to do for the rest of the afternoon?"

"Let's run by the office. I can show you how to enter and distribute the sales order."

Back at her desk, Rae showed Matt how to enter the order into the computer and create a work order for the installation of the equipment. Before calling it a day, she suggested that they stop in to see Dan, the division president.

"Hey, Dan, you got a minute?" Rae asked as she peered her head around the door.

"Sure, come on in," answered a man with a head full of dark hair that had the hallmark touches of middle age at the temples. The man was distinguished, yet his smile and demeanor were so welcoming that Matt momentarily forgot he was in the presence of his boss's boss.

"You remember Matt, don't you? We just completed his first week of training, and he just accompanied me on a sales call."

"That's great, how did it go?" Dan asked, directing his question at Matt, not Rae.

But it was Rae who answered.

"Good, for the most part," she replied. "Well, I guess not at first. The woman of the house voiced some reluctance, but I could see her husband was interested. I was able to bring them around, though. I threw in an automated climate control system, and it was just what I needed to close the sale."

"Interesting. I'm listening," Dan said.

"Go ahead, Matt, tell him how it turned everything around," she said, inviting her trainee into the conversation.

"Well, Rae is right. It wasn't looking good in my opinion. The lady even said she wanted other estimates and they should probably wait until after the holidays. Her parents were coming, and she didn't want the house to be under construction while they were there. I could relate to her and mentioned that my parents always have guests for the holidays and said something about the piles of blankets that my mom pulls out to make sure they're all comfortable. It's a mess, really, but ..."

"That's when I jumped in and offered them free automated climate control with the purchase of solar energy panels," Rae interjected. "That's how it's done, Matt. You have to recognize your opening."

"Good thing you did that, Rae—definitely upping the perceived value, as you put it," Matt said with a grin.

"Congratulations on your sale," Dan said. "It sounds like it was the perfect ending to a long week of training."

"It was, sir," Matt responded.

"I look forward to hearing about more successful appointments in the near future, Matt. I think you'll be a great asset to our company," Dan said, before adding, "Rae, if you still have a moment, I'd like to keep talking with you."

After Matt left the room, Dan pulled up a chair for both of them to sit.

"Congratulations on the sale, and congratulations on finding Matt. He seems to be a bright and ambitious young man," he said.

"If he sticks it out, I think he has a lot of potential," Rae commented.

"He mentioned perceived value, and then looked at you with a grin and sort of a smile. I'd love to hear more about that!"

"Well, I just shared with him that perceived value is one of the master keys to sales. That the art of being able to create high amounts of *perceived value* in the minds of the clients is key to making the sale. I tried to teach him that while you're selling a particular product or service, you want to make it more valuable to them, and throwing in something for free or at a deep discount is one way of doing that. I also shared that when people believe they are getting more value for their money, the offering becomes much more attractive," Rae said proudly, feeling confident in the training she'd given.

"I agree. Matt is lucky to have you training him. He is learning from the best at sales," the division president offered, giving her one of his genuine smiles that had been known to light up a room. "But Matt is not you, and we don't want him to be. Leadership is not about creating more versions of yourself. It's not about leading others to become like you or leading them in the way you want to be led. Leadership is about drawing out the best from within each person you lead and learning how to communicate and inspire others in a way that they are best led. You don't want to duplicate yourself. No, what you should strive to do instead is to duplicate the success you've had. I like to put it like this, Rae: leaders don't create followers; they create more leaders. I like to think of it this way: leadership is about bringing out the BEST in people, while teaching the 'systems' to add their own individuality to."

"That's a very good point, Dan. I never thought of it that way, but it makes a lot of sense!"

"It does, doesn't it? Before you leave, I do want to point something out that I'm not so sure you recognize from the conversation we just had with Matt."

"What's that?"

"Have you heard of the American actress, Lillian Gish?"

"I believe I've heard her name before, but I don't really know who she is," Rae admitted.

"She was a good friend of my family, and I'll never forget something she told me that has meant a lot to me over the years as I've led my teams. She said, 'I like it when people come back and tell me what I can do to improve; it's the kindest thing they can do for me.'"

"That is a unique way of looking at it. Is this your way of saying that you have something in mind that I can improve?" Rae asked.

"Well, I do have a thought that I think may add value for you. I couldn't help but notice a dominant word you said while recanting details on the sale you got today," Dan said.

"What word was it?" she asked leaning forward, obvious she had no idea what he was going to say and completely open to whatever it would be.

"The word 'I,'" her boss said. "I don't know how many times you said it, but it was probably close to a dozen. A good rule of thumb as a leader is shifting from thinking in terms of 'me' to 'we' in our conversations."

"Really? I had no idea I did this and surely didn't mean to make it all about me. Thank you so much for pointing that out."

"You're welcome, sometimes it takes a set of outside eyes to help us see what we can't. The truth is, I don't think it was a big deal to Matt because you made an incredible sale, and it was a great opportunity for him to see you in action. You took him under your wing and showed him the ropes—while making a tough sale. This scenario makes me think of the window and the mirror principle—have you heard of it before?"

"No, what's the window and the mirror?"

"When things go right, great leaders look out the window for who they can give credit to, and when things go wrong, they look in the mirror to accept responsibility. In this case with Matt, where do you see an opportunity with the window and the mirror? Is there anywhere you could have looked out the window to give credit to him for helping in the sale?"

"That's a good question, let me think about it for a second," she replied, staring right through a picture hanging on Dan's wall that depicted a buffalo running straight into a storm.

"I'm not sure, but as I'm thinking about it, something is coming to mind. I could have given him more credit when the sale was going south and he jumped in to share his personal family story. The family really connected with him on that. To think about it now, this was a huge turning point in the sale that I hadn't realized, and it was because of it that I was able to jump back in at the right time and close the sale. WOW, I see it so clearly now! How could I have missed this before?"

"I think you are right on point. One of my mentors, Brian Tracy, once told me that the number one key to success as a leader is a deep commitment to continuous learning and growing. You have been one of our company's top sales professionals for many years, and you've been the very top for the last two years—it's fun to watch you transition into leadership. You're going to be a great leader here with us," Dan said with a sincere smile.

"Do I have your permission to challenge you, Rae?"

"Um, sure," she replied with the slightest hesitation.

"It's kind of a tough one, but I know you can do it. I challenge you to delete the word 'I' from your vocabulary. Anytime you are going to use the word 'I' for any reason, even if feels weird not to use it, I challenge you to fill it with another word that's not one of what I call the 'I trio'–*Me, myself, and I.* Do this for the next seven days, and by this time next week, it will become a habit—a habit that I'm confident will serve you well for the rest of your life."

"Okay, I accept your challenge, even though I admit it might be tough. I didn't realize how much I use the word I until you pointed it out. I wish I had a recording of myself talking, because I'm still not sure just how much I do say it. But I'm up for the challenge–will you help me? If you notice the word 'I' come out of my mouth, will you give me a cross-eyed look?" Rae asked, half serious and joking.

"You bet," he laughed as he crossed his eyes in response.

Rae continued, "I've heard it said there is no I in TEAM. This is giving me a whole new perspective of what this means and how important it is. I have to tell you, this conversation is hitting me pretty hard, but I really appreciate it."

"As I think about it, I'm also going to get my Windex out and clean my windows, so I can look for opportunities to give credit to my team. And I'm pretty good with a mirror, but instead of focusing on how amazing I look," she smiled. "I am going to look for ways I can improve as a leader and where I can take responsibility for things that need to improve with people on my team."

"Sounds like a solid plan, one that will serve you and your team well!"

"Thank you for having this conversation with me. Sometimes I forget that what worked in sales doesn't necessarily work as a leader. Obviously, I have a lot to learn, but I thank you for taking the time to help and even challenge me. Keep it coming!" Rae responded with enthusiasm.

(3) The Four "Ings"

Matt officially joined the company's other sales representatives the next week. Some were veterans who had been in their roles for years. They were consistent performers, and among them were a few who had climbed the ranks, thus earning the best accounts and the awards that went with them. Then there were the newbies—the rookies who had no experience or were just coming into their own. Like Matt, they relied on their sales leaders to learn the ropes so they could begin their own journey in the company.

Leaning heavily on Rae, Matt learned some of their proven sales principles. Most of all, though, he learned the ins and outs of dealing with people, while presenting their products in the best light and in a way that appealed to their audience. In some ways, it was mind boggling, but Rae was skilled in presenting the information in an easy-to-understand manner.

Most of all, though, she was adept at building his confidence. Her goal was to get him out there after the two-week initial training, knocking on doors and making sales calls. When it was time, she wanted him to be ready.

As often happens, Matt spent a great deal of time with his peers — those who were in his shoes, learning the how-to's to being a successful salesperson. They had a lot in common, after all. They were studying their products and the features they offered, practicing their talking points, and discussing potential objections and the best way to counter them.

At the end of the two-week training, it was time to go live. The trainees would all receive an area to sell in and start receiving appointments scheduled by the company that would offset their efforts spent knocking on doors. They would also be selling solo, without a sales leader by their side. On the final training day, they had a celebration ceremony and were told, "You are ready. Your future is waiting."

Matt was ready. Oh, was he ready! In his mind, he was so ready that nothing could go wrong. How could it? He knew the sales material backward and forward ... he could recite the features of their offerings one by one and even knew how they were better than their competitors. Rae and the company had set him up for success—that was for sure. The rest was up to him.

"Are you good, Matt? Do you have any questions or concerns? I don't want to throw you to the wolves," Rae laughed.

"I am good. I'm looking forward to getting out there and applying what I've learned. Rae, I think I've got this. I feel really good about it."

"Okay, just remember, I'm here. Reach out to me if you have any questions or concerns. Believe me, it happens. And don't take the customer for granted. That will backfire, I assure you. My best advice is to be confident, but not cocky," she advised.

The next morning, Matt went out and started knocking on doors. He was expecting to get a lot of rejection, which he did, but was thrilled when he received a message with his first set appointment from the company. He was excited to have his first official sales call where the potential customers were actually asking him to come into their house. His confidence was tipping the top of the scales, and he was on cloud nine as he entered. From the minute he walked in the door, he was professional, and he knew he presented his sales pitch flawlessly, just as he'd practiced over and over and over again.

However, he didn't get a yes. He didn't even get a maybe. After spending an hour talking to the homeowner, he didn't feel like he knew the man at all or like he'd really even begun to break the ice, and he told Rae so.

"He was a tough sell, let me tell you. I don't think anyone could have sold anything to him—not even a free ice cream cone. I kept finding myself thinking, what would Rae do in this situation? How would you have handled this or that? But really, I don't think even you could have made the sale. I don't know why he wanted to meet with me at all. He had his mind made up before I even walked in the door," he said.

"Oh, man, that sounds tough. Don't beat yourself up too much; you're not going to get every sale. That's just part of the business. Don't let it get you down. Forget about it and move on," she advised.

And he did. By the time he received his fourth straight no from appointments that had been set for him, on top of his long hours spent knocking on doors, his confidence was waning. He was beginning to question everything from the training he'd received to his decision to even accept the job. Maybe he wasn't cut out for sales—after all, Rae had said everyone wasn't.

Feeling more than discouraged, he forced himself to go through the motions. By the time he walked into his sixth appointment, he had expectations—of failure, not success. Before he even opened his mouth and spoke the first word, he was sure the prospective customer wasn't going to sign on the dotted line.

Unfortunately, he was right.

At the end of the week, Matt sat at his desk, totally defeated. A few of his peers came in, and judging by their faces, he figured they hadn't had much luck, either. Sure, there were a couple who had gotten that all important first sale, but their rejections far outnumbered their sales, as well.

Not ready to give up, he turned to his sales leader.

"I don't get it, Rae. I've been doing everything by the book. I've been working really hard. I'm friendly, but professional. I knew my products and their features and benefits. Going into this week, I was so excited, I couldn't wait. By the time the week was over, I couldn't wait for it to be done. I'm sorry if I've let you down."

"Let me down? Far from it. You might find it hard to believe, but I'm actually proud of you, Matt."

"Proud of me! Why?"

"Weeks like these are tough, so much so that they are the reason many people walk away from sales. But you're still here," she smiled.

"I have to be honest. I'm discouraged and disappointed. I'm starting to think I don't have what it takes. It might even be best for both of us if I accept this now," he said, not even trying to hide the frustration in his voice.

"Whoa, wait a minute. Matt, I know this can be a super challenging job, especially at the beginning. But I also know that we can work on this together and turn it around. Look at me, Matt," she said. "You *do* have what it takes … and what you're going through is not only normal, but it's expected."

"What? Expected?! What do you mean?" he asked.

"There are different stages in sales, Matt—four actually. We call them the four 'ings,'" she started to explain.

"What are the four inks, or ings, or whatever you're talking about?"

"The four 'ings,'" she repeated, this time spelling the word. "Everyone goes through them, and I'd actually be more surprised if you didn't. Let me explain."

"The first stage is Forming. This is a learning stage, which is when your sales skills are being developed. That's what we've been doing for the last few weeks. In a way, you're still in the forming stages, because it's part of the process of working through to the next stage. Forming is a time when your confidence and excitement are high. You're looking forward to the unknown and the promise and potential it can offer," informed Rae.

"That sounds about right. But it's not real?" he asked, his interest in the conversation increasing.

"The phase is very real. It's a time when your confidence is high and so are your sights," his leader replied.

"That didn't last, though. So what's the next stage?" he asked.

"Forming leads to the next phase, which is Storming. But I want you to know that forming is always at play—you're always learning and developing … and that's a good thing."

"What do you mean by storming?"

"Storming is what you went through this week. You didn't get a sale, not one. You became frustrated, lost your self-confidence, and if I'm right, you're not very excited right about now," Rae called out the obvious.

"That's an understatement. It's not that I haven't worked very hard. I have. But no matter how hard I worked or what I did, I struck out every single time," Matt stated.

"It happens. It happened to me, but as you keep on pushing forward, the storm will eventually end. It has to. Just as there won't always be sunny days, there also won't always be dark, gloomy days. The quitters never learn that. They never get to experience those bright and sunny days because they give up. They don't wait the storm out, knowing that eventually the rejections become fewer, while their successes become more frequent."

"So right now, it's storming. How long does that last? How long before that turns itself around?" he wondered.

"Well, the answer to that question is up to you and how far you let these rejections and the disappointment in yourself set you back. It depends on how quickly you get back on the horse and face potential rejection again. The biggest question is how hard are you willing to work to turn it all around? These are questions only you can answer. But if you do what you need to do and 'Keep Buggering On,' as Winston Churchill puts it, the storming stage eventually leads to norming."

"What's norming?" Matt asked, this time with a small smile, as he followed the lingo.

"It's the third phase of the cycle. Think of it like a relationship. At first, you're forming—you're learning about each other. It's a time of discovery when everything is new and exciting. Then you get married, and one day, you discover it's not all a fairytale. You might even wonder who this person is that you married, and the relationship takes work. It's not easy anymore. But if you stick it out, you can work through it. You're invested in the relationship and committed to making it work. Eventually, you come to an understanding, accepting each other for who you each are—for better or worse, you might say," she laughed. "And your relationship adapts as you grow together and get to know how to work on it together. That's norming, and it consumes a great deal of your experience."

"Okay, I get that. So what's the fourth stage? The fourth ing?"

"It's performing—a stage when you're at your best. You've got it down, and you know precisely what to do and how to do it. It's at this stage that salespeople often find themselves becoming leaders who teach others what they've learned," she informed.

"Like you're doing now?" he smiled.

"Exactly, but it's a cycle, Matt. It actually repeats itself. You see, I've gone through the first three stages, and I've performed at a high level. But to be honest with you now that I'm a sales leader, I feel like I'm starting all over again, forming, storming ..."

"Wow! This makes a lot of sense. So you're telling me that my horrible week is normal, and you truly believe that I still have a chance?" For the first time, there was some hope in his voice.

"No, I don't believe you can. I know you can. Matt, the first day I met you, I watched how you handled making an unintentional oversight and immediately set out to correct it. I have no reason to believe that you aren't capable of turning this around and getting different results. Sure, your confidence has taken a hit, but there's only one way to fix that," she pointed out.

"What's that?"

"Keep working hard and go out there and get that first sale. KBO! Keep Buggering On, and don't quit! Take quitting off the table in your mind and watch as you break through barriers. Sales will come, I assure you. But it will be up to you to keep stepping into the unknown to realize your potential. Believe me, when it starts to connect for you, you'll be ready to take on the world. It's kind of like your matrix moment, if you've seen the movie *Matrix*, it's when time feels like it slows down and everything clicks. You know exactly what to do and how to do it. It's like magic. Your matrix moment will come as you keep moving forward and pay the price for it."

With Rae's support and assurance, Matt didn't give up. Instead, he buckled up, asked questions, and became even more committed to his success than he had been. It wasn't easy, but he went back out there and subjected himself to rejection. And he was rejected. But Rae assured him that being told no was par for the course—she told him to let the rejections be his vitamin, because every no brought him closer to that yes. She assured him that the worst thing he could do was give up, especially when he was just three feet from gold.

It didn't happen overnight. It took persistence and more than a little bit of internal coaching to keep walking back up to the plate for another strikeout.

He didn't even expect a sale when he walked into a home several miles out of town. It was a small, older home that sat on a couple acres. Owned by a couple who had three children, the family had outgrown the house, but explained that they liked the area and the privacy, so they decided to remodel the home and increase its square footage by building an addition onto the back. The homeowner explained that it seemed like the logical time to address other factors, like energy efficiency.

Matt found himself impressed as they shared their plans, and he spent a lengthy amount of time discussing their vision with them. He explained their systems and how they could be integrated, as well as the benefits that they'd receive for years to come. It was a productive and enjoyable back and forth, and the homeowners actually seemed to value his input.

That's exactly what he told Rae when he returned to the office.

"I have to admit, it was one of the easiest appointments for me. I mean, it didn't seem like work. It was more like I was talking to friends and, in the process, showing them how I could help them accomplish their vision."

"Great, Matt. So what's your plan? Are you going to follow up with them next week?"

"I can." Then he grinned and added, "But I don't *have* to. I got the sale! Rae, I got my first sale!"

"That's fantastic, Matt. I'm very happy for you, but remember, I always knew you could do it," she remarked.

"I know you did. But there were many times that I didn't, and your confidence pulled me through," he told her.

"I bet you feel great—you should."

"I feel like I'm on top of the world. As a matter of fact, I'm going to get back out there right now! Bring it on, Rae, I'm ready," he said, barely able to contain his excitement.

"Haha, I love your energy, and definitely get back out there! The best time to make a sale is right after you've made a sale! I can see your confidence isn't an issue," Rae laughed. "And I'm glad that you're ready to keep pushing forward with an exciting new attitude. But remember, although things are turning around for you, you're still going to face a ton of rejection."

"I know. But I think the worst has passed. I know I can survive the storm. I'm ready now for the norm," he smiled.

(4) Check Before You Correct

A Type A personality, Rae was a go-getter at work and at home. She'd always carried herself with confidence, rarely showing any hesitation or doubt in anything she did. And that was one reason she had become so successful.

Her home life mirrored that success. She and her husband had built their dream house a half dozen years before, and she took pride in making sure it was everything they wanted for them and their two children, Miley and McKay. A strong woman, Rae was keen on raising her children to be independent and ambitious, as well. She stayed on top of their education, making sure their homework was done and their grades were up to par, and they enrolled both kids in sports and other extracurricular activities to make sure they had access to different experiences as part of their development.

But it wasn't always as easy as she made it look. To outsiders, her life looked effortless, like she naturally had it all together, but there were times when she wasn't so cool, calm, or collected. It didn't happen often, but occasionally, something would trigger her one weakness, which was impatience. She was always able to recognize and correct it after the fact, mostly because it was one of her father's most unfavorable traits. Also a successful man, Rae's dad was admired by many in the community. There was no lack of people who looked up to him. But he placed the high expectations he had for himself on his children, as well, and when Rae and her siblings fell short of those expectations, he had a tendency to become a bit explosive. Those were uneasy moments in her childhood home, and at times Rae resented her father for not being more flexible and understanding. However, it was her father who pushed her to demand more of herself and at times, her children.

Wanting to be the best she could be at whatever she did, Rae always attempted to make sure she didn't repeat her father's mistakes. Her daughter and son knew that, no matter what, they had her support and love. But there were rare occasions when she would have a knee-jerk reaction that she regretted.

That morning had been one of them. After pouring her kids their juice and a bowl of Frosted Flakes, she turned to Miley and asked, "Oh, honey, do you need me to pick you up after school today?"

"No, I'm not staying late," her daughter replied.

"You're not? Didn't you ask your Algebra teacher for a tutor like I told you to?"

"I'm not going," Miley flatly replied.

"What do you mean you're not going? I didn't *ask* you if you wanted tutoring, Miley, I *told* you that you needed to get tutoring so you can pass your class. You may not care about math, but things will get way harder for you if you fail this class. And you deliberately defied me, and that is not acceptable. Fine! If you won't do it, I will call your teacher today and make sure it happens."

"But Mom …"

"No excuses, Miley. You had your chance. Get your stuff and get ready for school. I don't want to hear another word. And you can forget about going to the movie with your friends this weekend — you'll be studying!"

"That's not fair!" her daughter screamed as she rose from the table and stomped down the hall.

Rae's exasperation stayed with her until she got to work. Walking through the office, she noticed that Matt's desk was empty. Looking at the clock, she saw that he was late, but then she remembered that he had an appointment with a potential client that morning. It was a promising prospect and could potentially be a large commercial account … if Matt played his cards right.

"Good morning, Rae," their receptionist said. "Hey, Matt left a voicemail to let you know he's going to be late this morning. He said he'd talk to you when he gets in."

"Late? Well, I know he has an appointment. I'm sure that's where he is—it better be where he is," Rae muttered under her breath when she walked away.

After completing a virtual sales leaders' meeting, Rae called the school and left a message with Miley's Algebra teacher, wondering if her whole day was going to be conducted via voicemail. Sighing, she turned to her computer and tackled her monthly report, which kept her occupied for the rest of the morning.

It was lunchtime before she walked out of her office, only to find Matt walking in at the same time.

"There you are! How did the appointment go?" she asked with excitement.

"I didn't go. Didn't you get my message?" Matt asked.

"I thought you meant you were going to be late coming in because of the appointment. What do you mean you didn't go? I jumped through hoops to get that set up for you, and you canceled the appointment? Oh, please tell me you didn't stand them up! Matt, I'm very disappointed. What's wrong with you young people? Nobody follows through, and nobody thinks anything of it!"

"Rae, I can explain," Matt said, evidently embarrassed and upset that he was being called out in front of everyone.

"There's absolutely no excuse for blowing what could have been a really promising account," she said before spinning on her heels and walking straight into Dan's office.

The smile that crossed Dan's face when she walked through his door disappeared very quickly. It was obvious that something was bothering her—this wasn't a social visit by any stretch of the imagination.

"Well," he said, clearing his throat. "Judging by the look on your face, today is not going according to plan. Want to tell me what's going on?"

"That's an understatement. First Miley, and now Matt," she sighed.

"Whoa, back up. Start from the beginning," he said, leaning back in his chair.

"I had words with Miley this morning for not following through. And now I find out that Matt took the morning off when we had an appointment booked for him with the Urban Farm development south of town. What's with the kids nowadays? They don't have any accountability and don't care about the consequences. Now, I have to figure out what to do about Matt … and I'm left trying to salvage the relationship with the developers."

"I can see that you're upset, and maybe you should be. But did you ask Matt why he canceled the appointment?" Dan asked.

"Yes, I'm upset. Aren't you?" she replied, not answering his question.

"Well, it feels a bit premature to be upset. I don't know any of the circumstances yet. Why don't you fill me in?"

"Dan, there is really no excuse. He knew this was a big prospect. I thought he knew how important this was, and I feel like he doesn't even care. I don't know what's going on, but our conversation wasn't a good one."

"Okay, let's talk through this. Have a seat. Tell me what you know about why Matt missed the appointment today."

"He just didn't go, and the reason doesn't matter to me!" she said firmly.

"I can appreciate that. You have always operated from a no-excuse mindset, which is part of what has made you so successful. May I offer a couple suggestions?"

"Yes, please do! I am at a loss here."

"One of the biggest opportunities I've seen for leaders is related to how they give corrections. In fact, the more important the conversation, the less likely we are as leaders to handle it well. Most leaders tend to get trigger happy and blow themselves up with their own ammunition. It's like pulling a pin on a grenade and throwing it at their own feet. It doesn't end up well as they lead their teams. Most leaders launch into correction mode with their team, *before* they've earned the right to do that," Dan pointed out.

"Are you saying that I haven't earned the right to call it like I see it with my team?" Rae fired back.

"No, that's not what I'm saying, but hear me out for a second. If it was really as bad as you have played it out to be in your mind, then you would be right. I'm just not sure if this is the case yet. Here's my question for you. Again I have to ask you, do you know why he didn't go to the appointment?"

"Well, no, but Leonard from Urban Farms could only meet this morning because he was busy the rest of the week. I know this because I'm the one who talked with him to secure the appointment. So Matt must have changed the appointment, and I'm pretty sure we will never get their business after missing the appointment today. This infuriates me—we were right there, all he had to do was show up!"

"Well, this might be true, but at this point, these are just assumptions, aren't they? We don't know if this is really what happened or not, unless I'm missing something. If you are going to assume, I challenge you to assume innocence."

"What do you mean, assume innocence?"

"As a leader, before launching into correction with someone on our team, it's definitely in our best interest to pause, start with assuming innocence and, in this case, assume that Matt has worked it out with Leonard, rather than automatically assuming that Matt blew him off," Dan said.

He continued, "Well, oftentimes, leaders assume the wrong thing.

Instead of learning what happened and why, they jump right into correcting what they perceive to be wrong, this happens every single day with leaders all over the world. From experience, I can tell you that very rarely goes well. I've also learned that when we assume innocence, most of the time, we are right. Not every time, but certainly most often."

"Rae, there's a concept I'd like to share with you. Given today's circumstances, I think this is a good time."

"Okay. Actually, I'd really like to know how you would have handled this today, Dan. Because honestly, I'm just not sure how I would have done it any differently."

"You bet, there's a simple tool I call 'three checks before you correct.' Basically, there are three things that every leader should check before correcting members of their teams. If they don't check these three areas, it usually leads to defensiveness or resentment toward their leader. I learned the hard way that I was throwing grenades at my own feet, blowing up my ability to lead the people on my team because they wouldn't listen to me."

"Really, you have struggled with leading your teams? Must have been years ago, because everybody loves working with you."

"Well, thank you, but it didn't start that way for me."

"Okay, if you think it will help, I'll give it a try. Walk me through these three checks!" she said as she settled down into her chair.

"The first thing to check before correcting is ourselves. We should ask ourselves what is my motive or intent in correcting? Are my motives selfless, driven by a sincere desire to be helpful to this person? Or is there perhaps something else going on here, possibly coming from a different place—maybe a place that makes it known that we are the boss and that we have the upper hand? Our intent will always drive our results, and the people on our team will react to it," advised Dan. "This can be a tough one sometimes, Rae, because it requires leaders to do an honest assessment of themselves ... and if their intent is misplaced, it is the leader who needs correction."

"Hmm, that's interesting. I never looked at it that way. But I think in this case, I can check that box. I hate being on people's cases and correcting people, and I am not trying to have a power trip on this one with Matt. Based on this first check, I feel good about how I handled this today."

"Okay, fair enough," Dan nodded.

"So what else do I need to check?"

"Well, we all need this, it's not just you. Now we flip the coin. First, we check ourselves. Then we check them—checking on what I call 'the vital few.'"

"What do you mean by the vital few?" Rae asked, now seeming more interested.

"Let's dive into it. The vital few are simple areas to check as leaders to best understand the people we lead. I like to think about it in this way, it's kinda like when we go to the doctor. They do a physical version of this when they get a new patient. They get a baseline of their health by checking their vitals and asking a lot of questions. They would never prescribe anything to correct a condition before they know what that condition really is, so they do a thorough examination to make sure they've identified the real problem and suggest the proper remedy for it," Dan said. "Prescription without proper diagnosis is malpractice. A doctor would lose their license if they went around writing prescriptions to people without a proper diagnosis."

"I see what you are saying, that makes sense. But how does this apply to this situation with Matt?"

"That's a great question. Now, in my experience, I've seen so many leaders—myself included more times than I'd like to admit in my career—go around writing bad prescriptions to people they lead without a proper diagnosis. For example, any time we draw conclusions based on assumptions, without getting to know the situation and the people involved, we run the risk of giving out bad medicine to the people we lead, by making definitive judgements without the facts. The truth is as leaders, we can easily lose our ability to influence the people we lead, which can have long-term consequences with our teams and the results we are able to produce.

"The vital few are three key areas that are important to check in order to properly diagnose how we can help the people we lead. The three questions put very simply are... 'Where's their mind at, where's their heart at, and what are their feet doing?'"

"That's interesting. How do I figure out the answers to these questions?" she asked.

"Another good question. It's simple, really. You ask. Sit down and have a meaningful conversation and get to know them better. You might think you know them, but you might be surprised by what you don't know.

"For the mind, a couple example questions are so simple that some people might dismiss them. Questions like, how's it going today? Or, what's been on your mind lately? Or even, how are you showing up today? Then you listen carefully. You can learn a lot about where their mind is in this way.

"For their heart, you want to ask them about what makes them tick! What gets them out of bed in the morning? What are they passionate about? What do they dream about? My mentor, Brian Tracy, would ask me, 'Dan, what one thing would you dare to dream if you knew you could not fail?' I loved that question, and it drove me to dig deep and revealed what my heart longed for."

"I think I'm getting the mind and the heart, but what do you mean by feet?" Rae inquired.

"Their feet refer to their actions. What type of results are they getting? To find out why they are getting those results, look closer at what they are spending their time on. What does their calendar look like?"

"You see, it's more than understanding their goals, fears, and circumstances—you also need to review their actions. Are they doing the right things? Perhaps they aren't, but there might be a reason. I've found that the mind and heart control the feet. So if the feet aren't moving, or they are headed in the wrong direction, it's almost always an opportunity with their mind or their heart. Maybe they don't yet know exactly what to do. That falls back on us as leaders, and it means that instead of correcting, we need to be better teachers."

"This makes a lot of sense, Dan."

"It does, doesn't it? When you know what's in their mind, their heart, and their feet, you can come from a position of strength, knowing how to be helpful to them. That's why for doctors, giving a prescription without proper diagnosis would be malpractice. The same is true with us as leaders."

"Before we move off of feet, it helps to put ourselves in their shoes and experience their perspective. Good old-fashioned listening to their needs. It might provide answers we didn't consider, and I promise, these vital checks always provide good insight into how we can help the people we lead before launching into correction mode with them. I know it's opened my eyes every time I go through this exercise with someone that I lead."

"This is pretty incredible and seems to cover just about everything. I can't possibly think of anything else to consider before correcting someone," Rae admitted.

"You're right, that covers most of it, but there's one more area to check ... Check the expectations you have set. If they don't know what is expected, they can't possibly meet those expectations," Dan said.

"That makes sense, too," Rae agreed, before sharing an insight spurred on by Dan's words.

"Matt and I have only been working together for a few weeks now, and if I'm assuming innocence, as you put it, he tried to reach out to me this morning, and he did leave me a message at work. I bet he didn't want to bother me outside work, so that may have been why he messaged me on my office phone. I think this hits directly into setting clear expectations. I would have preferred him texting me on my cell phone and updating me there. But now that I think about it, I might not have told him that. I am seeing how my lack of setting a clear expectation could have added to our lack of communicating. I'll make sure he knows he can ALWAYS text me or even call me anytime he needs to on my cell."

"You totally get it, Rae," Dan acknowledged. "It is exciting to watch you learn and transform into a leader. I especially admire the way you are quick to correct yourself."

"Thanks to you, Dan. But I can see that I've still got a few things to learn, so keep these sessions coming. I can't wait to have this conversation with Matt. Hopefully, we can work through it together."

Dan nodded with confident approval.

"I know this will work out for you. I believe you'll make things even better with Matt as a result of what happened today. And I think the team will be stronger because of it, as well."

"Oh, but there's something I want you to remember. As you work on implementing this, it's important to not get overwhelmed by it all, and to keep it very simple. These checks can be done very quickly. Do you have the right intent? Do you know where their mind's at, their heart's at, and what their feet are doing? And have you set clear expectations with them? If you know the answers to these, you are in a position to offer valuable coaching and teaching and even correction, if needed, with those you lead, without risking writing them a bad prescription."

"This takes time, of course, but it becomes easier with practice and the better we know our people. Also, you'll get better at this over time, so don't be too hard on yourself as you start applying this stuff. Leadership is a marathon, not a sprint. If you're not making mistakes, you're not learning or leading."

"There is one final key to the three checks that is super important; we can't leave it out. Once we have a clear diagnosis, it's time to prescribe … If we don't make corrections when correction is necessary, we are being selfish and care more about ourselves than we do about the other person."

"Selfish, really? I'm not sure I'm following."

"I know, claiming it would be selfish not to correct someone probably seems like it's coming out of left field, doesn't it?"

"Yeah, left field is a good way to put it."

"Let's take a closer look. The question is, why would we not give correction when it's needed?"

"Well, maybe we're worried about how they will take it? It's uncomfortable. We don't want to be the bad guy."

"You're hitting the nail on the head," the senior leader said.

"Wait! I get it! We're making it about ourselves—we're being selfish!"

"Yes, we're more concerned about the other person blaming us for pointing out their deficiency than we are in offering them the guidance they need. We don't want to be the bad guy, so we shy away from the confrontation."

"Wow, I've definitely not thought about it like this before. And I see what you're saying. So if we've checked all three boxes and correction is needed, you're saying we have a responsibility to correct that person. If we don't, we are being selfish because we're making it about ourselves. Is that right?"

"Yes, exactly, you get it. The main takeaway here is that the very best leaders slow down for a minute before correcting someone, but then are willing to have the necessary conversations when needed. I've learned that this little extra time and attentiveness to check ourselves can go a long way in successfully leading our teams. My Wyoming cowboy friend, Pappa Hyde told me, 'If you take the time it takes, it takes less time.' That's something that I'll never forget, because it is so true."

"Thank you, Dan. It's obvious that I have a few unchecked boxes to tend to … and an overdue conversation with Matt. Wish me luck," Rae said as she walked out the door.

That afternoon, she met with Matt and took the time to hear him out. It turned out that Leonard from Urban Farms was the one who rescheduled the appointment with Matt for the next morning because one of his investors unexpectedly visited town. More than ever, Rae realized she was the one who had needed correction, not Matt. And she told him so.

Later in the afternoon, Rae found herself at her desk thinking about the day. She couldn't stop thinking about how Dan practiced what he preached with her. It was obvious that his intentions were to help her. He assumed innocence, asking a ton of great questions to understand exactly where she was at and why, then checked to see if he had already set clear expectations. Since he hadn't, he focused most of the time teaching her how to deal with these situations as a leader so she would know how to handle it better the next time. Rae learned a set of critical lessons that day. *"I've got a lot to learn,"* she thought.

Her next thought surprised her: *If I'm being honest with myself, I didn't really think I had a lot to learn—I really only thought I had a lot to teach.*

It was at that moment that Rae realized that she had jumped to conclusions with her daughter that morning, too. She didn't know what was going on with Miley—she hadn't even asked. Instead, she went straight to correction with her. It looked like she needed to go home and have her third meaningful conversation of the day.

(5) The Two L's of SELLAN

Fired up and excited to start a new day, Rae entered the office with a fresh attitude. After reflecting on her conversation with Dan, she realized that his experience and insight continued to transform her life both personally and professionally. Knowing that one day she could be as instrumental in her team's success as Dan had become to her over the past few years, she not only welcomed his advice, but was eager to apply it.

She had even applied his "checks" with her daughter, Miley, and was surprised to learn that she had, indeed, talked to her teacher about a tutor. After apologizing, telling Miley she was sorry for yelling at her and not taking the time to listen, the two had a much-needed heart-to-heart talk.

Rae learned that Miley's teacher informed her that a tutor was available two days a week; however, Miley opened up and told her that the tutor was another student—one who she admitted with embarrassment that she had a small crush on, and she didn't want to be embarrassed by how little she knew about the subject.

Learning that Miley was self-conscious shed a new light on the situation. Instead of being disappointed, Rae felt compassion and understanding. This is what Miley needed, not judgment, and it went a long way in strengthening their relationship.

It was a new day and one that brought another first. After new sales teams spent their first month in the field with Champion Solar, they were brought back in for two full days of training. Here they would receive instruction on the most important areas of sales to succeed within the company and in the industry.

Rae had attended these trainings before and had been asked to teach at many of them, but this was the first time she would be responsible for overseeing the training. She was well prepared—when it came to sales, she was an expert. Sales training was in her wheelhouse and put her in her comfort zone, perhaps for the first time since she had received her promotion, which came with all new leadership roles and responsibilities, recruiting, coaching, mentoring, and working to duplicate herself. Today, she wore a different hat, but knowing Dan, Josh, and Paul would be helping her during this event, she felt calm and excited.

The "Sellan Bootcamp" was strategically timed so that those attending would have enough experience after one full month in the field to be primed and hungry to learn more at a deeper level. In the span of two days, they would be immersed into the core philosophies, principles, and skills needed to succeed at Champion Solar. The tradition started 18 years before by the founders, Cory and Cameron, who wanted to ensure their culture was deeply embedded into the organization as they grew. Having participated in the training since taking on his role at Champion, Dan continued to be one of the key presenters years later.

The agenda was divided into three segments. The morning of day one was centered around training on the company's core philosophies, and Rae asked Dan to teach this. There would be a special activity during the afternoon session. Scheduled to be held offsite, this activity was designed to anchor in some of the principles taught in the morning. Day two would be a full day of critical skills training, presented by Rae and two of the top leaders in the company.

Dan was the face of sales in the company, and Rae was excited for him to kick off the Bootcamp. They would learn more about the company culture, what the company believed in, and some of the foundational sales principles that had rocket-fueled the organization's success in sales. Because these principles came from the top, she thought they would have the most powerful impact if they were taught by those at the top.

Initially, when Rae stood in the front of the room, she felt a little intimidated, but managed to keep any uneasiness under wraps during her welcome speech. "Today, we have an incredible training prepared for you. I encourage you to be all-in and play full-out to get the most out of this training."

"You've all known Dan from a bit of a distance, since he has been very busy working on an important project for the company for the past month. I wanted to give you a gift today and give you a chance to get to know Dan. He is the most influential leader I have ever had, and we are lucky to have him as our Division President."

"Thank you, Rae, it's great to be here with you and the team today.

Let's start with talking about the word 'sales.' Does anyone know where the word sales comes from?"

There wasn't a peep from the team as they all looked toward each other for a response.

He continued, "Our reputation at Champion has been built on the power of this word. It comes from the Old English word 'Sellan,' which means 'to give.'"

"Let's take a close look into what makes 'Sellan' so powerful and how it can help us continue to fulfill our mission in the years ahead. The original and intended meaning of sales—Sellan is our secret sauce, and applying it is what sets us apart from our competition. To help you understand the word, it helps to break it down. Let's start with the 'Two L's of Sellan.'"

Rae jumped in, "When Dan taught me the 'Two L's of Sellan' years ago, at first I thought they were nice ideas and made sense, but I had no idea how deeply impactful they would be in my life and in my day-to-day work. I can say that I attribute my success as the top salesperson in the company over the past couple years to the relentless application of the 2 L's. Trust me, I don't say this lightly. They have had a profound impact for me, and I know they can for you, as well. Okay, back to you, Dan—sorry, I just wanted to share that with the team."

"Thanks, Rae, glad you did, and please jump in anytime," Dan said.

"So with the meaning of 'Sellan' in mind—which means what again?"

"To give," Ryan answered.

"That's right. So the question becomes what do we give to our customers, and from there, who are we trying to benefit. Are we focused on helping them get what they want and need, or are we focused on our commission?" Dan asked.

He continued, "What gives sales a bad reputation is salespeople trying to give themselves what they want, at the customer's expense—their primary interest being in their commission."

"The 2 L's of Sellan are key principles that remind us to put the customer first, and how we can do it in a way that serves them first! I call these principles Lollipops and Lemonade!" Dan chuckled.

"Now I know what you might be thinking—lollipops and lemonade? Has this old man lost his mind? Well, that might be the case, but hear me out for a minute. Let's take a closer look at lollipops first."

"A man named Drew Dudley first introduced the lollipop principle. Dudley tells the story of an interaction he had at college with a girl who was waiting in line with her parents to register for classes as a freshman. The young woman was filled with apprehension and doubts—after all, the first year at college can cause a lot of anxiety. She was at the point of turning to her parents and calling off her plans of attending school right when Dudley showed up."

"Dudley came bearing lollipops, and he was passing them out to the people in line to spread awareness about a charity he was supporting. When he approached this nervous girl, he turned to the guy in front and said, 'You need to give a lollipop to the beautiful woman next to you.' The guy's face turned a shade of deep red, and he took the lollipop and begrudgingly held it out for the young woman to take. Dudley made a few more humorous remarks, and everyone in the line fell into laughter, even the nervous freshman student."

"The young woman claims that her life was forever changed in that moment. Surprisingly, she had this overwhelming sense that everything was going to be okay. Four years later, the now graduated woman told Dudley how greatly he had impacted her life that day. To heighten the sweetness of the story, she is now married to the guy who handed her that lollipop."

"This interaction was a life-altering one for this young woman. She made the decision to continue with college because of a moment that lasted less than a minute. Knowing how much of an impact his gesture had, Dudley was so inspired that he has now made it his life's mission to tell this story, his 'lollipop moment.'"

"Creating lollipop moments is all about being a day maker for people. When our focus is on being day makers, it changes how we show up for the people around us. It opens us up to be more alive and interested in them, which leads to greater productivity, higher fulfillment in our work, and as a result, more sales."

"If I could give you some time-tested advice, it would be to have lollipop breath, not commission breath. If there is a sales killer, it's having commission on your breath. Oh, I know commissions are important to you … and they should be. But your commissions are not important to potential customers … and they never will be."

"I challenge you to not make the mistake of pushing a product to get a commission. If you make it about helping real people solve real problems, you will receive the commission you need to be able to achieve whatever you are personally pursuing—whether that's to make money to pay the bills, invest, buy a car or a house, or take a vacation. Helping people solve problems will bring you whatever it is that you are wanting and needing, and when you do that, you make people's days and there is no ceiling for you."

Drew, a team member, chimed in, "Okay, I'm in—I'm going to start keeping lollipops with me all the time!"

"That's awesome, and it will be a great reminder for you to live this principle," Dan said.

Rae interjected, "It is so true. When I started thinking about how I could be a day maker for people around me, focusing on how I could create lollipop moments, everything changed. I found that my true success came as I started thinking in terms of what I could *give* to my customers and by helping them get what *they* wanted. I learned that when we make it about what we want, we're not likely to make a sale and nobody wins. But when we make it about them, a lot of times we can help them out with our products, and everybody wins! So if you find yourself with commission breath, I want you to do one thing—wash your mouth out with soap!" Rae's smile was followed by her contagious laugh. "That's right! I know it's kinda funny, but I'm also being kinda serious."

Dan added, "Think about it like this: what do you do if you smell someone with bad breath? You back away, right? Well, nobody likes stinky commission breath, and if they get a whiff of it, they'll back away from the sale just as quickly as you can say 'commission.'"

"Alright, I think you get the point. Now, let's dive into how lemonade is a secret key to sales success. And no, it's not about what you're probably thinking—the old adage of turning lemons into lemonade—although that's definitely good advice."

"Consider that you are invited to a friend's house for lunch. It's a hot day, and you'd love something cold to drink. Lo and behold, you see a large pitcher of freshly squeezed lemonade on the table, and you watch as your host fills their glass. But they don't offer you any. Finally, you ask, 'Can I have a glass of lemonade?'"

"Your host is taken aback and seems surprised when she replies, 'Oh, I am sorry. I was afraid you might not like lemonade, and I didn't want to offend you by offering you something you didn't want. I didn't want to put you on the spot and make you feel obligated to accept a glass.'"

"Now, that sounds ridiculous, right? Of course, most of us would offer a friend a glass of lemonade! But what if it wasn't lemonade we were offering, but it was still something they might actually want … but we don't offer it because we don't want to put them on the spot? Well, it's not too different from the way we hesitate to offer the incredible services we have to customers—services that are far more valuable to them than a glass of lemonade."

"What happens more often, though, is that we are reluctant to offer that glass of lemonade to our clients. Perhaps it is because we are afraid that we're being too pushy, but often it's because we are protecting ourselves from rejection. Oh, how we dread the word 'no,' don't we? In our minds, we could even think that by offering more, we might actually risk losing the entire sale. While those scenarios are understandable, experience proves otherwise. If people want or need a glass of lemonade, they're going to be grateful that you offered it to them. That glass of lemonade might be the one thing you have to offer that makes you stand out among the competition. Take a moment to think about that."

"We have found that those who take action, and are willing to open their mouths, who are willing to offer our 'lemonade' to people are those who find the most success. It's not rocket science; it's the simple science of human relationships," Dan continued.

"I challenge you to always be willing to offer the glass of lemonade. And with the lemonade, think about it being a disservice to them if you don't give them an opportunity to learn how we can help them. How can we offer them a better experience—a better solution? When given the opportunity to know what we can do for them, many people will not only take us up on it, but they'll also be very grateful to us for providing it to them. The best salespeople take massive action and are not afraid to open their mouths—and they're not awkward or annoying about it. Instead, they approach it with the mindset that they're helping their clients and giving them something they really want, just like a cold glass of lemonade on a hot day."

Rae jumped in, "When we don't take action, we don't have a chance. We miss 100 percent of the shots we don't take. It makes me think of one of my favorite quotes from Og Mandino in his book, *The Greatest Salesman in the World*, 'Happiness may not be the fruit plucked by my action. But without action all fruit dies on the vine.' It's true—when we put ourselves out there and take action, offering the lemonade, we may not get a sale out of it, but without trying, we don't have a chance. And if we don't get the sale, it's because the person didn't want lemonade, not because we didn't offer it to them. No harm, no foul. Nobody loses."

"I think we can all agree that lollipops and lemonade are great," Rae continued. "They are the two L's of Sellan, and we should never go on a sales call without them."

Dan piped in, "You see, lemonade isn't a sales killer. Now, let's move on to a principle that I think will benefit everyone in this room."

"I'm curious, you've been out there working hard on the streets, you know this better than anyone—what do you think the number one sales killer is? What's the one thing that kills more sales and destroys more success than anything?" Dan asked, looking around the room.

The team offered random guesses: "Not listening to clients' needs," "Poor communication," "Being afraid."

"Fear," someone answered.

"Fear is right," Dan announced. "Fear is the one thing holding us back from taking action. For that reason, I would be doing you a disservice if I didn't talk about it today."

"Most of you know that I've been around for a while. Over the years, I've learned what it really takes to succeed in sales, and in life, for that matter. Over the course of my career, I've discovered that fear is the most common reason people don't succeed. For that reason, I challenge everyone in this room to learn how to master my all-time favorite sales principle: Pluck the FUD."

Pausing, Dan looked around the room to gauge the team's reaction. Once he saw that he had their undivided attention, he continued.

"That's right. I said pluck the FUD. And getting good at this one thing is the reason high performers perform at the level they do."

"You're probably wondering what in the heck I'm talking about. Pluck the FUD? What in the world is that? Well, the best way I can explain Pluck the FUD is that it's kind of like when you're growing a garden. You plant rows of vegetables, and what's inevitably going to creep into the garden that you don't want?"

Amanda shouted out, "Weeds!"

"Yes, that's right, Amanda. Weeds are going to creep in. It's inevitable. And all it takes is for just one weed to find its way between those rows, and it'll overtake all the good stuff. Weeds are a garden killer, so when we see them, we've got to get in there and pluck them before they destroy the whole garden, right?"

"Well, the same thing happens with our minds. Weeds creep into our thoughts every single day. It happens to me. It happens to you. It happens to all of us, especially when we're pursuing our goals. Weeds work that way. They show up as thoughts like, 'Who do you think you are?' 'Get real, you can't possibly make that many sales,' 'You're a nobody,' and thoughts like, 'You're not as good as so and so!' Our minds are all guilty of being weed ridden from time to time. And even if we know deep down that those weeds aren't entirely true, they will, over time, choke out everything else. The good thoughts are 'cans'—I've got this, I can do this—while the weeds are the cant's in our mind. And if we aren't diligent about pulling those cant's out of there, they will overtake all the good stuff."

Danielle's arm rose in the air.

"Yes, Danielle?" Dan asked.

"I get what you're saying, but what do you mean by pluck the FUD? I mean, what is FUD?" she asked.

"That is a great question! The most common weeds we all face are FUD," Dan replied as he turned to the whiteboard and wrote the three letters. "FUD is an acronym for Fear, Uncertainty, and Doubt. FUD plagues all of us, and when it does, we've got to get it out! We've gotta pluck the FUD!"

Rae jumped in and said, "I'm no stranger to FUD. In fact, I've experienced a ton of FUD throughout my sales career, and to this day, I still do. The key is recognizing it when it presents itself and then knowing how to get rid of it. I'll never forget when I was much like you, only two weeks into my job here, and I hadn't even made one sale. Not a single one. It was so bad that I was almost fired. I was out of money and hope. Even my parents doubted me—they told me to quit and move back home. Oh, the FUD was real, so real that I had pulled my suitcases out and was ready to pack. But luckily, I didn't end up quitting. And I have Dan to thank for that. He taught me about his success secret over the years and how he learned to pluck the FUD. Yep, as successful as Dan has become, he also had to deal with FUD. But Dan actually did something about it, and it works. He showed me how to get rid of FUD using what he calls the Fearless Formula™. It was a game changer. To this day, it still is. I'll leave you with that for today, but you can count on us talking more about the Fearless Formula™ in the coming months."

"I agree with Rae. You'll definitely be hearing more about the Fearless Formula™ as time goes on. For now, what's important is that you recognize that FUD is going to creep into your mind and getting rid of it is absolutely crucial to your success," Dan added.

"If you focus on it, it will get bigger and take over your brain. It's just like in nature with a garden, what you tend to and focus your attention on is what will grow and thrive. If you tend to the weeds, but not the plants, they will grow like crazy. The same is true for your thoughts. If you focus on the fear, uncertainty, and doubt, they're going to grow stronger and stronger. So you want to get in and Pluck the FUD as soon as you can. Get rid of it early and get rid of it often!"

A quick glance at the time told Dan that the morning session was nearing its end. "I hope you can see how the principles you've learned so far today can have a positive impact on your success here—and in everything you do. Remember to bring lollipops to every sale and offer your clients the lemonade. It's good stuff!" Dan concluded. "Tomorrow, Rae will go into specific tools and strategies that you can use to help people get what they want, but I wanted to introduce some of these key ideas as a foundation for you to build on. Thank you for being such an attentive audience this morning. I appreciate your time and participation."

"I'm confident that each of you have the ability to be successful. Our job is to help you do just that. Before we break for the morning, though, I want to leave with you what I believe to be the seven most important words in sales: *It's not about you; it's about them.* Serving others is the cornerstone of our success, and we believe it will be key for your success with us, as well. That is why we are taking you offsite this afternoon for a hands-on experience to anchor these principles in. It's one way we like to instill our values in our team, planting what we believe will be seeds that will set you up for long-term success," Dan said. "Let's meet back here in an hour. Until then, lunch is set up in the conference room. I hope you enjoy it."

(6) The Seven Most Important Words in Sales

Dan was no stranger to sales or leadership. He had owned a solar company for more than two decades, and he had managed to grow the business over the years. Sure, there had been tough times—the construction industry had taken a swift downturn a decade before the country's economy took a nosedive. Still, the business endured, and 15 years later, they had not only survived, but were thriving. Without a doubt, part of that was due to the fact that people were being more energy conscious than they'd ever been, but many people attributed the company's success to one thing—their leader, Dan.

A profitable and growing company is an attractive asset, and Dan received a few offers to purchase his business. While some of them were appealing, Dan wasn't interested in selling—he'd built the business from the ground up, and he was invested in it, his employees, and the community.

Five years later, though, Dan received an offer that interested him.

Champion Solar wanted to buy his small business, and they were willing to pay a respectable amount for it. That wasn't enough for Dan to consider selling, until Champion conditioned the offer on the fact that Dan remain on their payroll as Division President for the company. After a great deal of research, they knew the business was a good investment, but the key to that value was its owner. If they were to successfully expand, they would benefit from the knowledge, experience, and success that Dan brought to the business.

After several months of negotiations, the deal was sealed, and Dan was no longer a business owner, but now an employee. It was a win-win for Dan and Champion Solar. Champion greatly expanded its territory and gained the expertise and leadership of a proven business owner, and Dan had the opportunity to expand his influence on a much larger scale, as he would now be making decisions that impacted far more employees, and he'd also be able to instill his sales and leaderships principles across the country.

Dan never regretted his decision. Champion Solar gave him the freedom, actually, it was their preference, to maintain his leadership style and values in his new role. He could continue to do what he loved until he was ready to hand over the reins when he was ready to retire. Until that day, he knew the business he had worked so hard to build and grow would continue to function under his principles and philosophy.

But he wasn't ready to retire just yet. Although his three children were grown and starting families of their own, Dan enjoyed working and wanted to continue to do so for several more years, at least until his wife, Sheri, would retire from teaching at the local grade school. Traveling was in their plans in the future, but for now, they were content staying where they were. They were very community oriented, and their lives revolved around their kids, their church, and the town where they'd built a home and a life.

Social responsibility had been important to Dan long before it became the trendy thing to do. In fact, it was during their leanest year that he instilled the value among his employees. While his business managed to stay above water, there were many businesses that closed their doors during that time, resulting in an increased number of families seeking assistance. During their slow months, Dan gave every employee the opportunity to take a day off with pay to make a positive impact on the community, and 100 percent of his employees took advantage of the opportunity. The good part was that Dan let them select their own cause. Food pantries, veterans' associations, nursing homes, pet rescues, churches, and organizations like the Salvation Army all benefited from their contributions. It was such a success that first year that it became an annual initiative that the employees looked forward to every year. Dan practiced what he preached, and not just one day a year. He volunteered to work with at-risk teens and youth groups, a role that came naturally to him after raising three kids and being a Sunday School teacher for many years. He also had volunteered as an early morning seminary teacher for four years—teaching high school students every morning before school for an hour to help them kick off their day by learning about the Bible and Jesus. He received a calling to be a leader of a church congregation, volunteering in this role for four years, and later an area authority, volunteering for this position for eight more years. His service to the community and his church had always been highly rewarding endeavors for Dan, ones which enabled him to make a difference and impact the lives of many current and future leaders.

The first day of their sales bootcamp was a continuation of that effort. During the afternoon, the sales team would be taken offsite, where they would get firsthand experience in serving, not selling. Not only did it tie into his values and beliefs, and those of the company, but it enforced what Dan deemed to be the most important success principle available to any salesperson—selfless service.

"This afternoon, we will be taking a field trip of sorts," Dan explained when they returned from lunch. "We won't be attending a networking benefit, and no sales will be involved. In fact, they aren't allowed. That's because this afternoon is not intended to benefit you in any way; it's all about how you can benefit others."

"The Sellan Bootcamp would not be effective or complete without going out and putting into action some of the principles we have been talking about. We will be doing service. In fact, selfless service is an acronym of Sellan. The 2 L's are Lollipops and Lemonade, and the S is Selfless Service. You'll learn the rest of the acronym tomorrow."

"Rendering selfless service, being useful to others, is a key to applying the *most important words* in sales. The key is making it truly about them, and not about you," he said, placing strong emphasis on the phrase.

"Those words are the foundation this company was built on, and they've continued to support our vision and philosophy and our success throughout the years. Starting today, we hope they will become ingrained in your minds and hearts and will bleed into your work ethic."

Dan explained that the team would be taken to a homeless shelter, where they would assist other volunteers with sorting and handing out food and clothing donations, processing requests for assistance, and even assisting with completing employment applications and writing resumes. The shelter assisted the homeless with their basic needs, but it also directed individuals and families to the services they needed the most. It was Dan's preferred charity for the sales bootcamp because it gave them a unique experience that was not only enlightening, but humbling. In this environment, there was no room for selfishness—it was, indeed, all about others.

Four hours later, the company van returned them to the parking lot.

"Okay, everyone, let's all meet back in the conference room for a 30-minute wrap up," he said.

Ten minutes later, he took the floor and asked everyone to share their thoughts about the afternoon. The responses were not new—Dan had heard them before. "Until I saw it firsthand, I didn't know there was so much need," "It made me feel fortunate for what I have," and "I wish there was more we can do."

"Well, there is more you can do," Dan countered. "We can all do more. That is why our company gives you one day off with pay each year to volunteer for a cause of your choosing. It keeps us grounded and reminds us that we are here to serve, not just sell."

"You see, when we help people get what they want, we end up getting what we want. It's not about you; it's about them: as you adopt and apply these words in your sales career, you will see how far it will take you. These words are a game changer, so much so that they have been at the core of everything we have talked about and done today. Think back about what you've learned and the sales principles we've discussed in your first day in bootcamp. Sellan, the 2 L's, Lollipops and Lemonade, the seven most important words, and selfless service. They all have one thing in common, and that is that it is not about you—it's all about *them*. I challenge you to repeat these seven words in your mind throughout the day, *every day*. It takes self-discipline and awareness to keep pulling them into the forefront of your thoughts, but over time, they define your mindset. Applied consistently over time, your mind will naturally follow the principle, and it will prevent you from making the cardinal sin that undermines most sales—thinking, even for a passing moment, that it is about you or that it ever was. When these seven words become part of your waking consciousness, you'll have developed the mindset and skills of a master sales professional."

Dan's eyes swept the room to make sure he still had their sales team's attention.

"Just as you did today in your volunteer service, we invite you to put your customers' wants and needs before your own. As a company, we're committed *to giving* them what *they* want, not what *we* want for them. This is how we win over the long term. Experience has shown us one thing: we can serve others without selling, but we cannot sell without serving others."

"Today, you made the lives of some people better. In some way, no matter how large or small, you became a day maker. I know as you focus on the 2 L's of Sellan—finding ways to give people lollipops and lemonade—you will make a lot of people's days. And over time, by putting yourself out there and offering people what we have for them, you will experience success. But I don't want you to feel that the fact that you serve someone else makes you entitled to anything. You are not. Serving has its own rewards, many of which are not related to your sales, your goals, or your success. You are not entitled to success because you have been day makers, but being a day maker by serving others will help you create habits that attract others to you."

"I want to leave you today with a challenge. I challenge you to write these seven words in a prominent place where you will see them throughout the day, every day—write them on your bathroom mirror, the back of your clipboards, on Post-it notes. Send yourself texts or notifications or set alarms on your phone to serve as reminders of these seven words during your day. The more places you see them, the more they will be ingrained in your brain and thought processes, and the more you will approach every encounter, every potential customer, and every sale with this philosophy: *'It's not about you; it's about them.'* I know that as you embed these words into your mind and your heart, you will experience a ton of success. I'm living proof of this and Rae is, as well. So are many others who have come before you. Success leaves a trail; let it be a trail of service."

(7) Firetrucks, Baby Monsters and Mini-Dings

Rae was delighted to see that her sales team expressed eagerness the next morning. It was what she had hoped for when she had asked Dan to open the Sellan bootcamp, knowing that he had a knack for presenting policies and techniques in an easy-to-understand, even enjoyable, way. More than that, she appreciated the fact that he made them memorable. After all, who could forget things like lollipops and lemonade and the infamous Pluck the FUD? Never once had she had difficulty remembering them, and she hoped her team would have the same recall.

Rae's challenge was in making the second day just as memorable, enjoyable, and impactful. She was well aware that Dan was a tough act to follow. But today, she felt she was bringing in a close second with Josh and Paul. Twins, they had been at the company for 15 years, and not only had they enjoyed a reputation full of success, but they'd also earned the respect and admiration of their peers throughout the years. As a bonus, the two were so full of personality that people jumped at the opportunity to work with them.

"Yesterday was a fantastic introduction into sales, and it was specifically designed to lay a deep-rooted foundation for success: developing the winning mindset you need to succeed over the long term. Dan excels at that, and I thank him for taking time out of his busy schedule to help instill that mindset in us. Then, we broke things up a little and went offsite so we could experience what it was like to serve others without any selfish motives whatsoever. I hope you found that to be rewarding—I know I do, whether it's during these bootcamps or when I take advantage of my service day here at Champion to volunteer for a worthy cause or apply this principle in my personal life, helping with fundraisers at my children's school or giving a few hours of my time toward a bigger cause. I am confident that each of you will also adopt and own this principle. As a matter of fact, believing that you already hold these values was a non-negotiable characteristic we looked for in the hiring process."

"That brings us to day two of your first Sales Bootcamp. Yesterday was about the mindset for success, while today will be all about the specific strategies needed to take your skills to the next level, which I'm sure is of interest to everyone in this room," she said, noticing nods of agreement in her audience.

"Because I know all of you get the chance to hear from me often, probably more often than you want," Rae laughed, "I thought I'd change things up and let you learn from a couple different voices. Most of you know of Josh and Paul; they're both friends of mine and are well respected by their peers and supervisors alike. Yes, they are identical twins, but their personalities are not identical, I assure you. That's one reason I was excited when they agreed to join us today; I wanted you to see that you can be your authentic self, while still holding true to the universal principles they're about to share with you. Before I turn it over to them, I want to share their backgrounds with you. Both of them started as sales professionals, just the same as you. For the past 15 years, they've run one of the highest-performing teams here at Champion, consistently ranking among the top 5 sales managers in the company, among hundreds of our leaders across America. They are impressive, not only in their results, but as you will see in their size— at 6'5" and boasting 250 pounds of muscle, they tower over anyone. They are as highly respected as they are tall, and most of us know them affectionately as the 'Twin Towers.' While I don't want to give them too big of an ego," she chuckled, "I do want you all to give a warm welcome to Josh and Paul."

The men walked to the front of the room and introduced themselves, taking advantage of the opportunity to joke about being twins.

"I'm Paul. I'm the stronger one," the first twin said.

"I'm Josh, the better looking one," countered his brother.

"Seriously," Paul said, "we know it can be difficult at first to tell us apart. When you get to know us, though, you'll be able to spot each of us in a crowd. While we do look alike, we are also quite different. Just like you, we have our own unique expressions and mannerisms, and you'll catch on to those rather quickly. Right, Josh?"

"He's right," Josh told the group. "It's been a long time since we've been able to fool anyone for very long. Over the years, though, I think it's fair to say that while we are a lot alike, we each have different strengths. In the end, we complement each other well. In a way, you are all the same. You each have different strengths and can learn from each other and use those strengths to create results as a team that you can't always do on your own."

The two continued on, transitioning right into training as a team that worked like a well-oiled machine.

"I know you've been wanting to dive into skills training—because when I was in your shoes, that's what I really wanted. I wanted to learn how to sell, sell, sell," Paul said. "Trust me, that's what today is all about. But it has its place, and there is a reason why this portion of your training was saved for the second day. Rae absolutely had to cover mindset training first, starting with Dan's message about the 2 L's of Sellan and his unforgettable Pluck the FUD. Then came that incredible service trip focusing on the importance of serving people and living by the seven most important words in sales. These principles lay a foundation for the type of thinking that brings out our best, which in turn allows us to show up as our best and attract the best people who want to buy from us. I want you to listen closely—learning the skills is the easy part. The hard part is guarding our minds and taking action despite fear. Josh and I know it isn't easy. We've been in your shoes."

"We sure have," Josh agreed. "Rae mentioned that it was stated yesterday that you are experiencing a ton of rejection on a daily basis. Is that right?"

Heads nodded throughout the room.

"While I'm sure you would love a secret principle that makes rejection go away, there is no such thing. The truth is getting a ton of rejection is exactly as it should be in this stage of your selling careers. After a month in the field, every one of you has probably experienced more rejection than you have ever faced in your life in such a short period of time—and I wouldn't expect anything different. The good news is there are some things you can do to minimize and prevent a lot of rejection. There are also things you can do to overcome rejection when it occurs. Today, we are going to focus on those strategies. And we promise that after today, you will have a ton of simple ideas that you can apply to help you push past the rejection and generate more sales. Paul, do you want to get started?"

"Sure thing. Let's start with value scales. Here's how it works—let's say you have a balance scale and on one side is the value, and on the other side is the cost. If the value outweighs the cost, the customer's answer is almost always going to be yes! On the other hand, if the cost outweighs the value and tips the scale in the opposite direction, the answer is almost always no. That makes sense, doesn't it?" he asked, opening a PowerPoint presentation to demonstrate the principle.

"Nobody is going to buy something if they don't believe it is worth the price tag. Why would they? So, if you're getting too many no's, there's a reason, and it might be because your value scales are tipped too far to the no side. The good news is you can do something about it. Your job is to increase the value so the scales are tipped toward the yes side. The more you increase the perceived value to your potential customers, the more your sales numbers will increase."

"Rejection is a natural part of everyone's growth in sales," he explained. "The more rejection you experience and keep pushing through, the more successful you will be. Training sessions like this one have helped me learn how to navigate through rejection and come out stronger because of it."

He continued, "I want you to remember that it's *normal* to encounter rejection. That's true. It's also *normal* to 'self-talk' yourself into a downward spiral when faced with rejection again and again. It's normal to start thinking about all the reasons why you can't succeed because everyone around you is telling you NO. It's normal to hate rejection and want to do everything you can to avoid it. But there's something else that's important for you to realize—*normal doesn't lead to success.*"

"Now, you might think I'm crazy, but I want you to think of rejection as your friend. Yes, you heard me right. Rejection can be your friend. In fact, as Les Brown puts it, 'Let no be your vitamin.' In other words, let it fuel you. Let it energize you. Let rejection motivate you to stand up and proclaim that you're going to prove it wrong. It's what you do with all the no's that makes all the difference to your success. If you can hack your brain to think of rejection as fuel, and let it be your vitamin, it will go a long way to help you push through your fear and turn your action into success. In fact, 'No' is the N in Sellan! What you do with all the no's will either drive you toward your goals or drive you into the ground."

Josh jumped in. "Here's the thing, what Paul said about hacking your brain is spot on. If you don't tell your mind what to intentionally focus on, it will come up with *anything* to think about. This is mental suicide in sales. Mark my words, a wandering, unfocused mind is not a recipe for success."

Rae chimed in, adding, "Especially when people all around you are rejecting you and telling you to take a hike. What's your mind supposed to think when you get rejected? Oh, that's nice! No way! Of course, not. You've got to get in front of this and protect your mind by planting intentional thoughts. It's up to you to pluck the FUD, guard the door of your mind, and, yes, hack your brain and fill it with all the reasons why you can succeed, filling it with what you want."

Josh jumped back in. "Here's how I like to think of it, Rae. To pluck the FUD, you gotta hack your brain, you gotta give yourself a kick in the RAS—the Reticular Activating System. It's the part of your brain that focuses on things. It's kind of like the filter for our focus. Of all of the million different things we *could* focus on at any given time, the RAS is what helps our brain determine the one thing it *will* focus on. That's why there is so much power in setting clear specific goals and writing them down. I'm a firm believer in setting specific goals, especially when they're written down."

"This doesn't mean you should expect rejection or find ways to attract it, but you do want to anticipate that it will come and prepare yourself for it. Did you know that anticipation will give you a competitive edge? Think about it; when you can anticipate the objections you're going to face, you can prepare for them beforehand. You will be ready. This gives you the upper hand, and it helps you to be confident when you're addressing a prospective customer's concerns or objections."

Paul jumped in, "Here is one thing you can do to hack your brain, filling it with intentional thoughts that serve you. The secret lies in this little black box." Paul lifted the box so everyone could see it, showing that it was filled with well-worn 3x5 index cards. "Dan taught us this when we first started selling, and it's made all the difference in the world for us. This one brain hack alone has helped us to guard our minds, take action in the face of fear, and pluck a lot of FUD that we wouldn't otherwise have. This is one of the keys that we attribute to our success, and as you can see by the condition of the cards, we've used this strategy a lot."

"Here's how it works... You take a piece of paper, or a three-by-five card, and write out a specific thought, quote, or idea that gets you fired up and puts you in a state to become your best self. Carry this card with you while you are selling. Pull it out while you're walking between houses. The more you look at it, the more you will remember it. Memorize this thought, and it will start to become part of your waking consciousness."

"When you get rejected by someone, you are not thinking about how crappy you feel—you're thinking about whatever you have written on that card. You're thinking... *I know I have the ability to achieve the object of the definite purpose in life; therefore, I demand of myself persistent continuous action toward its attainment.* Or whatever you have written on your card."

"I challenge you to do this. In fact, here is a 3x5 card to help get you started. Let's do the first one together." Paul then led them through an exercise creating their first card.

Josh asked the group, "Does this make sense? Do you have any thoughts or questions so far or anything you want to dive into deeper before we move on?"

Matt raised his index card. "I think what I need right now is to learn how to overcome a few specific objections that I keep getting over and over."

"Great, let's hit these head on. Which ones are you getting the most right now?" Josh asked.

"Well, I'm getting a lot of people telling me they are interested, but they have to talk to their spouse. When I hear that, I almost groan because I know that the deal is dead, because coming back later has just been meaning goodbye forever. I haven't been able to overcome that objection at all—not even one time. And what am I supposed to do? What can I say to overcome that? It's not like I can say, 'Nope, sorry, you can't talk to your husband. That's not allowed.'" Matt laughed.

Jarrett also piped in: "I'm getting a ton of 'I don't have the money' objections, which seems to be pretty common, and also, 'I don't have the time.'"

"Oh, yeah, the infamous honey, money, and busy objections," Paul stated. "Josh, why don't you take this one?"

"I'll be glad to. Overcoming objections isn't as difficult as you think. In fact, it's really quite simple. If objections are your biggest challenge, listen up, because if you follow the next tip, things are about to go your way. In order to overcome objections, there's really only one thing you need to learn how to do really well—you need to get to know ELDN. Who's ELDN? Some people think of ELDN as the silent partner in the room—he's there, but you don't really know who ELDN is. Listen, you don't know enough about your customers if you don't know their ELDN. These are the four major areas of your potential customer that will tell you if they are a good fit for what you're selling. If they are not a good fit, you're wasting your time and theirs. And if you don't get good at finding ELDN, I guarantee you'll experience more than a fair share of rejection."

"Okay, I'm sure you're curious and would love to know what ELDN is. Simply put, ELDN is an acronym that stands for the four things you need to know that will tell you if you can help them out. ELDN is what seals the deal as a yes or a no," Josh continued as he clicked the remote to move to the next PowerPoint slide. "Let's dive into this a bit. E stands for their Emotional Reasons to Buy Now. What would drive their desire or emotional connection to what you are offering them? The L Stands for their Logical Reasons to Buy Now. This is what could justify their emotional reasons for wanting to buy. To appeal to their logical mind, a flash sale can do it, free upgrades, a deep discount, or giving them something extra at no additional cost could help justify their purchase—something that pushes them over the edge or tilts the scale more to the value side. The truth is, people buy based on emotion, and they justify their emotional purchase with logic. It's a one-two punch. People love to talk about a great deal they got on something that they are emotionally connected to—wanting to justify it."

"Moving on, the D in ELDN stands for their Dominant Reason for Avoiding to Buy. Not their dominant reason for *wanting* to buy—but their dominant reason for *avoiding* to buy. If there is any resistance at all to the sale, there is always a reason. What is the one dominant reason that's keeping them from purchasing? You want to learn their dominant reason as soon as possible.

"They aren't going to make it easy because they don't want you to know what it really is. Why? Well, let me see if we can illustrate with an analogy. Paul, you're up!"

Paul walked to the front of the room, carrying a shiny red firetruck in his hands.

"Join me as we take a trip to the toy store," he said. "Let's go back in time to when Josh and I were kids. I walk into a toy store and the first thing I lay my eyes on is this shiny, red, brand-spanking new firetruck, and I immediately start playing with it. To me, it's the best firetruck ever—it's the only one in the store and the only toy I want. Well, Josh walks in the store and sees me playing with this firetruck, and what toy do you think Josh wants? You guessed it—the firetruck I'm playing with, and I'm not about to give it up. No way. This firetruck is mine! As far as I'm concerned, he can have any other toy in the whole store, but he's not gonna get his hands on *my* firetruck."

A quick glance across the room told him he had the team's full attention.

"Now take that scenario and replace firetrucks with objections. Customers give us all the objections they have for not buying, but they won't easily give us their real objection—their firetruck. Most of the time, objections people give out easily are just smokescreens to try and get rid of us. What I'm saying is that customers don't want you to know what their real objection is, so they give you something else, some other objection."

"Your number one key skill is learning how to draw out their true concerns and learn their *real* objection. Learning to do this is one of your biggest opportunities and won't come in a day or through a simple training. It will come as you work hard over the next several months, and it will click naturally as you pay your dues. But in short, you have to learn how to establish a relationship in just a few short minutes with them. Your customer is not going to share their firetruck with you unless they feel like they know you, like you, and trust you. This can be done very quickly; in fact, it has to be done quickly or you won't be making many sales. If you can establish that trust, they will be more likely to open up to you and let you help them. Now, not every person who gives you the firetruck will buy from you, but if you can get them to give you their real objection, their firetruck, you'll know the truth about where they are and how you might be able to help them. Only then will you be able to see if you have the tools to overcome that objection. Now, I'm going to take my firetruck and sit down. Josh, why don't you take it from here, brother!"

"That was well said, Paul, I really like this firetruck analogy! There's a lot to unpack there, but I think we all get the idea pretty clear. Getting the firetruck can be tricky to uncover, and it takes the most skill out of all the skills we will be teaching, because people don't just hand out the real reasons they aren't buying from you. They keep their truth close to their chest, oftentimes because it can get pretty personal. If they feel like they don't know you, like you, or trust you, they are likely to throw something out at you like, 'It costs too much,' or 'I have to talk with my spouse,' to get rid of you. By the way, those are both smokescreens in this case."

"Let's move forward to lightly touch on the N of ELDN, which stands for their Need. What is their true need? What payoff will they get from our product that will compel them to purchase from you? There has to be a specific need(s), or they will not take action to buy."

"ELDN is key to successfully giving people what they want— "Sellan"— you've gotta bring ELDN out from hiding to really help people. When you help them, this helps you!"

"Knowing about ELDN is the first step, and it's already a lot for today. Now that you have been introduced to him, the second step will come over time as you learn the art of finding him quickly in a way that builds rapport with your customer. This is like magic."

"Listen, your biggest opportunity in overcoming objections lies in your ability to find our little friend, ELDN. For today, I just want to introduce you to this idea—we will dive deep into how to find him over the course of the next three months as we work together and as Rae and Dan continue training you. For now, I challenge you to keep an eye out for ELDN and see what you can come up with to draw him out from hiding in your customers' shadows."

"You know what else I've learned about objections? Okay, I'll tell you," Josh smiled and continued without waiting for an answer. "Objections are only questions in disguise. Early on, they aren't a big thing—they're nothing more than baby monsters. But guess what happens if you feed them? They turn into full-grown monsters. Every time you feed the baby monster, it grows a little. Before you know it, your baby monster has become bigger than life, and it will eat you alive! Here's what I tell everyone: Do. Not. Feed. The. Baby. Monsters."

"Now I know the little baby monsters are there, and they don't seem like that big of a threat. Still, it's hard to ignore them. But like the sign at the zoo that says do not feed the animals, don't feed the baby monsters! Don't feed the objections because if you do, they will grow and keep coming back and ultimately kill the sale."

"Here's how we feed baby monsters, and a lot of times without even realizing we're doing it. We create an environment for them to grow in by focusing on them, talking about them. They grow when we dwell on them or when we keep bringing their smokescreens up. We have to know when and how to keep the sale moving forward and avoid getting trapped or sucked into trying to resolve a concern that isn't real."

"How do you kill the baby monsters, Josh?" Paul challenged his brother.

"That's easy—mini-dings! And since the time we were kids, Paul has always been better at mini-dings than me, so I'm going to let him tell you how they work."

"Okay," Paul said. "Let's say you've got a baby monster in the room. Now, remember, your baby monster is an objection that was just thrown out to you, and you need to figure out how to handle that objection."

"One of the best ways to handle an objection and find out if it is a smokescreen or not is by using mini-dings. Let me explain what I mean ... How many of you have ever been to the fair or a carnival and played that game where you swing a gauntlet to try to ring the bell or raise the light to the top? You take your mallet or gauntlet and raise it over your head and bam! You swing it down as hard as you can, but you only get halfway. No matter how hard you try, you can't get the bell to ring or get that light all the way to the top in one swing. Can anyone relate?"

"Oh, yeah," Matt said, while others nodded their head in agreement.

"So what do you do? You figure out how to get to the top another way. Instead of going all or nothing on one swing, you give it a smaller swing, a mini swing, and you watch as it goes up. You keep on swinging, giving it little taps that raise it a little at a time—ding, ding, ding! Until a series of little dings and taps brings you to the top and voila! You've bypassed the baby monsters without feeding them, not stopping to address them along the way and manage to close the sale and everybody wins. Stopping to address concerns that aren't real is how you feed baby monsters. Also, assuming that a customer is going to have a specific concern that we hear a lot and putting undue energy toward them is another way we feed baby monsters. This is death to the sale, and nobody wins. When it comes to objections, you have to keep the sale moving forward, just like with mini-dings at the fair. Your job is to keep it moving forward, and your customer will stop you when they need a little more focus and attention, further explanation, greater clarification, etc."

"Paul's right," Rae interjected. "It's the little steps keeping the sale moving forward that will get you to the finish line. The Twin Towers know how to slay baby monsters, and they can spot a firetruck a mile away. Right, fellas?" she smiled.

"Well, maybe not a whole mile," Paul laughed.

"Fair enough," Rae laughed. "For now, Josh and Paul have given you some really effective strategies to start applying. They've used them, and their sales records tell you everything you need to know. I think we've covered a lot and given you all a lot to think about. Before we break, though, I want you to realize that you've learned all six principles that make up the Sellan acronym. Let's take a look."

With a click, she flipped to a new PowerPoint slide.

S•E•L•L•A•N
"To Give"

S – Selless Service
E – ELDN
L – Lollipops
L – Lemonade
A – Action Despite Fear
N – No (let it fuel you)

"As you can see, we've talked about every one of these principles. The S in Sellan stands for selfless service, which you got firsthand experience with yesterday. The E is ELDN—remember, you have to know your client's ELDN if you're going to overcome their objections. Then, we have the two L's: lollipops and lemonade, and you need to offer your clients both of them! Moving on, it's important that you take action despite fear—when fear creeps in, then you know what to do—Pluck the FUD! And we'll continue discussing strategies on how to do this in future trainings. Last, but not least, is No, a word most people don't like to hear, but it is a reality. Rather than letting it discourage you, however, learn how to let it fuel you. When you do, it will drive you closer to your goal."

"So, that's Sellan, and it's so important that this two-day training was centered around it. Do yourself a favor and memorize these six principles—even better, integrate and apply them in every sales appointment. When you do, you'll begin to see results," Rae encouraged.

"Perhaps this is a good time to close out for lunch. As we go on, don't let me forget to share with you a very simple three-part formula you can use to overcome objections. It's what I still use today as my mini-dings until I know I have a firetruck and have to spend time addressing a real concern. We will go much deeper into this as time goes on, but I want to take it one step at a time in a series of mini-dings that will get you to their firetruck and help you slay baby monsters. Till then, enjoy your lunch."

(8) Formula for Effective Coaching and Teaching

Over the course of the next six months, Rae watched her team learn and grow. While they still faced rejection, which was to be expected, she noticed that those rejections were increasingly countered with sales. The ratio of no's to yes's was definitely closing, but she could sense that not all members of her team were happy with the pace. The fact that they wanted it to happen faster was natural. It would be for anyone who had their sights on a goal and worked hard to accomplish it.

It reminded Rae of her son. McKay had been bit by the sports bug a little later than his friends. By the time he expressed a desire to play baseball, his friends and classmates had been playing for several years. Most had started very young, playing T-ball at the early age of four or five, and had then moved up in the recreational leagues. McKay, however, was in the fourth grade when he started playing, and to his discontent, he had a lot of catching up to do.

Of course, Rae and her husband encouraged McKay to be patient, and they were honest with him, letting their son know that he was going to have to work harder to catch up to his teammates. They played catch and threw pitches, giving him some much-needed batting practice, hoping to build confidence and help him find his groove with his swing. And for the most part, they had seen real progress. He was meeting the ball with the bat more consistently, most of the time; however, it was obvious that he was out of his comfort zone in a real game, when the pressure was on and his teammates were depending on him.

An overachiever herself, Rae wanted to help her son in any way she could. At every available opportunity, she grabbed a glove and took him to the park, where they'd practice the fundamentals over and over. It was what Rae knew to do—practice, practice, and never give up, because she knew that with time, her son would be hitting the ball more than he missed it.

But McKay didn't see it quite the same way. What started as an enthusiastic desire to play the sport ultimately became a chore. He found excuses not to practice, avoiding it when he could. Then, he transferred blame. Whenever he didn't play as well as he liked, he blamed it on the coach, the umpire, the pitcher, and from time to time, his parents were at fault—hearing them cheer him on from the stands made him feel self-conscious or embarrassed or rendered him unable to concentrate. Lately, it had gotten to the point that their son would refuse to listen when they gave him pointers or he'd become defensive whenever they tried to help him.

Her husband had suggested that Rae just let it go and see what happened.

"Back off. Maybe we are putting too much pressure on him," her husband suggested.

"I think he's just reluctant to admit that he could use our help," Rae countered. "You know, it's almost like he's not even listening when I'm trying to help him anymore. Maybe his pride is getting in the way."

"Or maybe he's becoming resentful. While we mean well, maybe he doesn't see it that way. Maybe he thinks that we're actually criticizing his skills," her husband stated.

A similar scenario was taking place among a few of her team members. While they had all made progress and had seen an increase in sales during the last six months, there were signs that they weren't as receptive to Rae's teachings as they once had been.

It was Matt who really surprised her. He had made great progress and showed real promise, but then he had a slow period—one that impacted his confidence and his enthusiasm. As Rae was working through it with him, she suggested he return to the basics.

"Go back to the beginning with everything you've learned. It'll help you pluck the FUD and get back into the groove," she said.

"That's not the problem," Matt stated.

"Well, then, what is the problem?" Rae asked.

"I'm not sure. But telling me to do the same thing I've been doing isn't going to help. I know it won't. Don't worry about it. I'll figure it out," Matt said, turning his attention to a spreadsheet on his monitor.

**

"I don't get it, Dan," Rae admitted the next time they met. "Oh, I know that there will be slow periods and dry spells. That happens. But Matt's always been very receptive to my advice. Many times, he was the one who sought it, looking to me for answers. This is the first time, though, that he's ever shut me down and pushed me away. I'm not sure if he really wants to try to overcome this entirely on his own, or if it's me. Could it be that he does want advice, but he just doesn't want it from *me*? If so, he should join the club—McKay doesn't want my help anymore, either."

Dan could see that the thought troubled Rae deeply, as he would have expected it to. After all, she took great pride in her success as a salesperson and was developing the same level of pride in her successes as a leader. He'd seen it before, and it looked like Rae was taking it personally. The last thing he wanted was for her to doubt herself.

"Before you go any further, I want you to know that I understand where you're coming from. I've been in your shoes, both here and with my kids and some of my Sunday School students. It's hard because we really do want to try to help," Dan agreed.

"You've been in my shoes? I would've thought that this would be foreign to you. You have such a way with people that I can't imagine anyone ever dismissing your advice. Most people readily seek it— me, for one," she said.

"Believe it, Rae. I'm no stranger to such scenarios. Just like every leader, there have been times when I tried to coach someone and it just didn't work. Even when I gave them the very best advice I could because I truly wanted them to be successful, there were times when they totally ignored what I had to say and times when they ended up resenting me for even trying to help them."

"What did you do? I mean, what can I do? I want to help—I truly do," Rae pleaded.

"Rae, you might remember when I talked to you about knowing the people you lead—knowing their mind, their heart, and their feet," he said.

"I sure do, and I've tried to apply that principle when I'm coaching my team."

"Well, there is more to it. Actually, there are four things to take into consideration. Responses such as those you've seen with McKay and Matt are what happens when any one of four essential ingredients are missing. If you have time, this sounds like a good time to go over them."

"Absolutely," Rae answered, leaning forward in her chair.

"Let me begin by saying that successful coaching results in someone being inspired by you, not deflated by you. I've found that there are four ways to do that, Rae. The first key is to align with them. Meet them where they are."

"What do you mean by that?"

"Listen, the starting point to helping somebody create successful change is to understand and appreciate their world. Have you ever asked yourself, 'Why can't I get through to this person?' Well, often it's because they feel like you don't understand or appreciate their world. You remove that possibility when you successfully align with your team."

"How do I do that?" she asked.

"Well, it's pretty simple, and you already know this, but it's worth reviewing. You listen to them. The magic is knowing what to listen for. Going back to what we talked about several months back, find out where their mind is. How are they showing up? Are they in their head or preoccupied? Are they operating from a place of abundance or scarcity? Are they a victim right now, or are they a creator?"

"Ah, yes, I recall. Go on," Rae invited.

"Next, find out where their heart is. Do you know their specific goals and what they're passionate about? Do you know what they dream about? Do you know why they get out of bed and show up to work on your team? Do you know what their feet are doing—meaning what their calendar looks like? What constant actions are they taking, and what are the results they're getting? The answer to these types of questions will help you successfully align with your team and meet them where they are, which is the first key. Listen, try influencing someone without meeting them where they're at. I think you'll agree that it doesn't go well."

"Okay, align with them. Got it," Rae affirmed. "What's next?"

"Number two is to lift them. You have to know when and how to lift the people you lead. To lift someone you lead in a way that is meaningful to *them*, I invite you to follow the platinum rule," Dan advised.

"The platinum rule? I don't believe I've ever heard it."

"Now, I know you know the golden rule, which is to do unto others as you would have done unto *you*. But the platinum rule trumps the golden rule. In the platinum rule, you do unto others as they would have done unto *them*. In other words, what works for you might not work for them. How do *they* like to be lifted? Perhaps, they prefer positive words, a quick note, a private text, public recognition, or maybe just time with you as their leader? Find out how they like to be lifted, and take the time to make sure the people you lead feel valued and appreciated by you. Call out the amazing work they are doing in a specific area or have them share what they're doing with the team. Do whatever works for *them,* and find a way to lift the people you're leading."

"Interesting. I never thought of it that way. So, what's next?"

"Next is to challenge them. But be careful how you do it. You want to challenge them directly, with their permission. Otherwise, they might become resentful, and we certainly don't want that. We haven't succeeded if the result becomes resentment. We align ourselves with our team and understand where they're coming from. Then, we lift them — letting them know how much we appreciate and value them. This foundation is needed before delivering a challenge that's well received. Only then will they appreciate a direct challenge from you. And even if they don't appreciate it, they will at least respect it and gain a greater respect for you. There's a difference when a challenge is offered with an intent to be helpful, even if it's direct and maybe a little hard to hear. If they feel like you care about their success, they will appreciate the challenge. If they feel like you don't care about them, or they feel you are insincere, they will reject what you have to say, and likely resent you."

"Oh, it's becoming clearer. You've challenged me many times! And as I think about it, you ask me for permission before you do it," Rae interjected.

"I learned that a long time ago from Art, one of the most powerful leadership coaches I've known. He taught me what I call the golden question, which is, 'Do I have your permission to challenge you?' Believe me, getting permission to challenge someone is a game changer. They become more receptive and less likely to resist what you have to say."

"Oh, I won't forget that, especially now that I know why!" Rae exclaimed.

"Last, but not least, we have the fourth ingredient for successful coaching and teaching, and this one might surprise you," Dan forewarned.

"What's that?"

"Get out of their way. Don't be a hover boss. Don't be a helicopter parent. If the first three ingredients are there, get out of their way! Allow them the opportunity to make mistakes. In fact, make it a mantra within your team—we make new mistakes!"

"I thought my job was to help them, every step of the way."

"It is, but if you've done the rest, you've got to let them walk on their own. It's like our kids, Rae. When they ride a bike, we teach them everything we can, and we hold on while they try it out a few times. But sooner or later, we have to let them go to see if they can do it on their own, without our help. That is our ultimate goal—to coach them and teach them to successfully reach their goals on their own! In fact, some of the best leaders are those whose teams feel like they don't need them. I know it sounds counter intuitive, but when they don't need you, you have done your job. Listen, leaders don't create followers, they create more leaders."

"Some of your team members might be ready to fly solo and think you don't trust them because you won't let go. Others might need you by their side, with your thumb on the pulse of things a little longer, but you won't know that until you let them go. To be the most helpful to the people we lead, we have to be willing and able to get out of their way."

"Rae, as you align with the people you lead and get to know them, you will know when and how to lift them, you will know when and how to challenge them, and you will know when and how to get out of their way. Don't underestimate this—there is power in these principles, and they work. I've applied them over the years not only with my sales teams, but with the teens in my youth group and with my own kids. You probably didn't even notice it, but I've applied the same principles with you—and see how well that turned out?" Dan smiled.

"Thank you, Dan. And now that you point it out, I can recall a time or two when you might have been applying these principles. And I have to tell you, I can already see how they might be useful in my own home," Rae mentioned.

"Oh? Anything wrong?" Dan asked.

"It's just that I'm used to being a parent, but lately, I've taken on the role of a softball coach, and I'm afraid it hasn't worked out very well. And in looking at these principles, it's apparent to me how I'm definitely part of the problem. It's just that it's a tough look in the mirror. I've never considered that it's me who needs to change, especially as McKay has shown obvious resentment lately when we practice. I've just been blaming him."

"Well, just your awareness and acknowledgment of this is a really big first step in the right direction. Try it with McKay and see what happens. Most of all, I encourage you to apply these four principles with Matt and your team. I'm confident they will help you successfully coach your team!"

(9) The Four Laws of Leadership

Dan had taught Rae the formula for effective coaching and teaching, and in implementing it, she realized that she didn't know her team as well as she'd thought.

Over the course of the next week, she scheduled meetings with every member of her sales team, setting aside two hours of one-on-one time with each of them—time she hoped would help her understand them, their goals, their needs, and their fears. By unveiling those things, she hoped she'd gain some insight into how she could best support them in their growth.

Her first meeting was with a young sales member on her team who Rae was eager to get to know better. Coral had been with the company for nine months, but for some reason, Rae didn't feel like she knew her much better than the day she'd first walked through their door. It wasn't that she was aloof or standoffish—no, in Rae's eyes, the young woman was reserved, even a bit timid, and Rae was determined to get her to open up. She hoped their conversation would help her make some headway toward that goal.

And it did. At the beginning of their meeting, Rae reviewed her progress with her. Coral was doing well, but it seemed her sales had plateaued and then leveled off. That wasn't unusual, in fact, it was common, but she had hoped Coral would have been able to create an uptick in her sales by now. The fact that she hadn't reassured Rae that this meeting was necessary and, hopefully, would help them discover what they could do together to turn things around.

"Coral, I want to apologize. I should have held this meeting with you months ago. Getting to know my team is important to me. I want you to know that you can come to me when you need help. So, how about we get to know each other a little better?" Rae smiled.

"Sure, what would you like to know?"

"Well, tell me about yourself. What did you do before you joined us?"

"I worked at a law office," she answered.

"Oh, that sounds interesting. What did you do there, if I can ask?"

"I was a receptionist and an assistant. I answered the phone, prepared legal documents, and met with clients to gather information, that sort of thing," she offered.

"That's quite different than sales," remarked Rae. "So, why the career move?"

Coral squirmed uncomfortably in her chair, and for a second, Rae regretted making her uneasy. She was just about to switch the subject and put her at ease when Coral answered.

"Well, it's not something I'm very proud of, but I was let go," she said meekly.

"I'm sorry to hear that, but I'm glad because you joined us. Do you want to talk about it? You don't have to."

Coral hesitated for a moment before answering.

"No, it's all right. Officially, I was told it wasn't a good fit. But I think it was my personality."

"How so?"

"Well, I've always been friendly, but I guess in the law office, that was out of place. You see, I'd talk to our clients and listen to their stories, but the firm wanted someone at the front desk who was very professional. Personal conversations were off limits. But when people see an attorney, it's usually for a reason. They wanted to share what's going on, and they wanted to know that we were going to help them."

"I can see that," Rae nodded.

"Well, the lawyers didn't see it that way, and they let me go. To be honest, I took it personally. I guess I still do."

"Coral, I hope I'm not overstepping my bounds, but from what you've told me, you might not have been a good fit—not for that environment, anyway. But I have to say it surprises me. In the time I've known you, you come across as quiet, even cautious at times."

"I think that's intentional, Rae. I don't want to make the same mistake twice. I need this job," she replied.

"And we need you!" Rae smiled. "From what I'm hearing, though, what wasn't a good fit in your old job is a strength, a benefit, if you will, in sales. Opening up to customers and being able to comfortably converse with them is a major part of building relationships. Coral, what was considered a fault in that job is a strength in your career with our company. I think this could be a pivotal realization that could make a huge impact on your career."

During the rest of the meeting, Rae worked on getting her young saleswoman to open up. As she did, Rae saw a Coral she hadn't seen before. The young woman had a genuine gift in being able to put others at ease and making them feel comfortable. They had such an enjoyable conversation that, for a few minutes, Rae almost forgot that they were having a business meeting.

At the end of the meeting, Rae knew that she needed to help Coral pluck the FUD. Her former employer had planted uncertainty and doubt in Coral's mind—doubt in herself. With Rae's encouragement, she knew that she could overcome that self-doubt, and when she did, Rae was confident that she would be a strong presence on her team.

Her meeting with Matt was also an eye opener. While she felt like she knew Matt, she discovered that she didn't know very much *about* him. To that end, their meeting was very fruitful.

From the day they'd met, Rae knew she admired Matt. He was considerate and had a wonderful demeanor. She'd found that he was dedicated to learning and growing, a quality she really admired. But once again, it was what she didn't know that surprised her.

Matt wasn't shy about sharing his goals. He wanted to be one of the top salespeople in the company. But there was one problem. Matt was impatient—he wanted to be at the top *now*. As Rae talked with him, she discovered why. Matt had more than a professional goal—he also had a personal goal, which he told her was to be financially secure enough that he would be able to support a family … when he found the right person. He told her about Tessa, his former girlfriend, and shared that he had suffered setbacks that had impacted their relationship. He was determined to turn his financial situation around, and he'd given himself a deadline to do so. The problem was his goals were lofty and his timeline was unreasonable. As a result, he was dealing with frustration and disappointment—in himself.

Rae learned that no one was harder on Matt than Matt himself. It was easy to see that he demanded more of himself than anyone else ever would, and it was even easier to see that when he didn't live up to his own expectations, he was his own biggest critic. Beating himself up was one of his specialties, and it saddened her to see such an ambitious young man put so much pressure on himself. Setting such high expectations was commendable, but the inability to consistently meet those expectations could have a very negative impact on anyone's career.

It was a fine line between encouraging goals and feeding his competitive spirit and helping him see that his success was a journey—it couldn't be attained in one giant leap. If he tried to, he would risk disappointment and becoming a self-proclaimed failure, and likely give up.

That wouldn't do.

But Rae also discovered that Matt was very much like her. She could see that he was an overachiever and willing to go the extra mile to be successful. That was a strength, but from her own experience, it was also a fault. She remembered too well the days, years even, when she was so consumed by her success that everything else diminished in importance. Looking back, she knew that it was Dan who helped her see that she needed balance, and when she created it, she found that it helped her in her career. To help Matt realize this, she simply needed to replicate what Dan had taught her. Her leader had already given her everything she needed to help her team. It would be up to Matt to accept that help.

Like looking in the mirror, she could sympathize with Matt. She'd been there, demanding more of herself than anyone ever expected of her. Perhaps that was why she had been the top in sales for several years in a row. Perhaps that was why she was chosen to be a leader.

But Rae hadn't wanted to be a leader. On the contrary, she had been quite content and happy being a top performer in sales. If anyone asked her, she would have denied any interest in taking on a leadership role. When she was approached about it, she wasn't shy about expressing her reluctance—initially. In her viewpoint, there was no reason to throw away a successful career—one she'd worked hard and long to achieve. And for what? There were no guarantees that she'd be a good leader. But after some prodding, Dan helped her to see the opportunity in a new light.

She could remember the day well.

"Listen, Rae," he'd said, "sales is the short game—one that you've played well. You've mastered it, as a matter of fact. But there's no leverage in selling personally. Leading a team is the long game. Leadership gives you an opportunity to duplicate yourself and multiply your efforts. This enables you to create leveraged results where you can enjoy real long-term success."

His words gnawed at her until, ultimately, she realized that Dan was right. But still, it was a huge step, and there was no guarantee that she would succeed. After all, she'd never been a leader and didn't even know where to start. She hadn't had any training, so she had no idea what to do or how to do it. But Dan believed in her and committed to giving her the support and help she knew she needed.

Knowing she had him as a trusted mentor, she took the uncomfortable leap and accepted the position.

Dan had been a fantastic mentor and advisor, always patient and fair-minded. Yet, he was always willing to tell her exactly as it was, without mincing words. She noticed early on that he had a way of being direct with her in a way that she felt that he cared about her. Rae appreciated knowing that anytime there was a problem, he would address it with her head on.

Still, she realized there was so much for her to learn. And she had been right. Sales and leadership were very different—being good at sales and being good at leading a team took two very different skillsets. Like most sales leaders, Rae had been promoted into leadership because of her high performance in sales. But it quickly became apparent that being great at sales wouldn't mean she'd jump straight into being a successful leader.

Dan was a tremendous help, and time and time again, she found herself not knowing what to do, but finding she could model after his leadership style that had been so effective with the people he led. His style was one she'd always admired; it brought out the best in her. It was her hope that she could take everything Dan taught her and make it her own, so she could bring out the best in her sales team.

The individual meetings with her team were part of that process, and when she talked to Dan the next week, she told him so.

"I really feel like I've learned so much about each person, Dan. Actually, I'm surprised. I truly thought I knew them, but I had just scratched the surface. Now that we are getting to know each other better, I really think I can be a much more effective leader, and I'm confident that they'll be so much more receptive to my efforts," Rae confessed.

"I'm not surprised at all," Dan countered. "I had the same experience when I was first entrusted with a leadership role. I liken it to the fact that just as our sales teams need to build relationships with customers, we as leaders need to build honest, sincere relationships with our teams. We can't do that unless we know them—their goals, their passions, and their fears."

"You don't say! I finally feel like I have a solid foundation with my team, one that we can really build on."

"It's just part of the Four Laws of Leadership. Without these four laws, everything we've talked about up to this point would crumble," Dan stated.

"Wait! I've heard you mention the Four Laws of Leadership before. I meant to ask you about it, but it's been so busy. Do you have a few minutes to talk about it right now?"

"Certainly. But before we start, I have to warn you, these laws are kind of like a crown on top of everything I've learned over the years as a leader. Are you ready for this?"

"Are you kidding me! You've been holding out on me!"

Dan laughed. "No, I've just been waiting for the right time to talk with you about it. In fact, we would need a little bit of time to really dive into these to do them justice. Also, these laws don't mean as much without the foundation that you've been laying with your team. So I think the timing is good to talk about them now."

"Okay, let me send a quick text to free up some time and grab my notepad," Rae said.

"Alright, Dan, I'm all ears," she said when she was done.

"Okay, it's important to know that the principles we've already considered together as you've been building your team are critical to the success in putting these laws into play. Things like the three vital checks, the window and the mirror, align-lift-challenge-get out of the way, and all the leadership principles are what make the four laws so powerful."

"Now, the first law is: *the people you lead have to know you have their best interest at heart.* Let me ask you a question to go a little deeper on this. Rae, what do you think would happen if you really didn't have the best interest of someone on your team at heart? What would happen to your ability to influence this person? Would they be able to feel this from you?"

Dan answered his own question, "I've found that people are pretty intuitive, and we can tell when someone really doesn't have our best interest at heart. It doesn't take long for this truth to leak out of us in a lot of ways. Rae, we've all been there—there are times when we're working with someone who's a real piece of work, but here's the thing. If you can't figure out how to care about them, don't fool yourself into thinking you're going to effectively lead them. Sure, you'll probably be able to get their compliance, but you won't get their commitment to go the extra mile."

"Most leaders care, but that's not enough. Here's the real secret of this first law—the biggest challenge leaders face is: *do the people they lead know that they have their best interest at heart?* Do they know it because they experience it? The real magic is when genuine caring bleeds into all company communication, all policies, and all interactions, positive and negative. Is it experienced, even when they're being reprimanded? When this happens, the power of this first law is in effect."

Rae was head down, furiously taking notes.

"Is this making sense?" Dan asked.

"Oh, yes, I'm loving this and tracking with you, keep going!" Rae said.

"So let's go to the second law. *They have to know that you trust them.* If you don't trust somebody that you lead, your ability to influence them goes to the floor! Think about it like this, have you ever had a leader that you didn't really think trusted you? How did that work out? How impactful was their leadership for you? Did you find yourself resistant to them? Were they successful when they tried to coach you or correct you? Probably not, right?"

"Listen, Rae, I challenge you to not fool yourself into thinking that you can effectively lead somebody that you do not trust. When you find yourself not trusting someone on your team, you need to ask yourself some very tough questions. The starting point is to turn inward and ask yourself, 'How am I the problem?' Now, you'll probably think to yourself, 'What? I'm not the problem! They are the problem, and that's the problem!' I get it. But if you don't trust this person, what are you doing about it? Have you been radically candid with them? Have you had the needed crucial conversations? If not, why not?"

Although silent, Rae was listening intently.

"If you have had these conversations and it's not working, why are you allowing them to remain on your team? Maybe that's how you're a part of the problem. If you are not willing to have those crucial conversations and be straight up with the people you lead, then you can consider yourself a huge part of the problem—having this human being on your team that you don't trust."

"Here's the reality. In most cases, I've found that having crucial conversations with people results in trust being restored. Not all of the time, but most of the time. And sometimes the only way forward is to break that relationship, unfortunately."

"I'm thankful I haven't encountered that yet," Rae admitted.

"Just know it is a reality every leader will face, sooner or later. Okay, moving on, the third law is that *they have to know you have confidence in them*. I've seen you express this with your team. It's powerful! Have you ever had a leader that you knew had confidence in you?"

"Yes, definitely," Rae answered.

"Now let me ask, how did that confidence invite you to show up? Think about this for the people you lead. Your belief in them will make them want to succeed for you. They want to prove you right, and that will take them far. Now, I know you might not have full confidence in someone, and in that case, you can work on it. Find small wins. Where can you be confident in them? What are they great at? I've found what Goethe, the ancient philosopher, said to be very powerful. 'If you treat a man as he is, he will stay as he is, but if you treat him as if he were what he could and ought to be, he will become what he could and ought to become.' Give them a name and a reputation to live up to, clearly communicate expectations with them, and demonstrate your belief in them and watch them step into that greatness."

"And, if they're not stepping up—or if they're just not great at what you need them to be, it's time to ask yourself some tough questions, like: what are they doing on my team? That's on you! You have a responsibility to take decisive action."

"And here's the last of the four laws: the people on your team have to believe that you would take a bullet for them—not literally," Dan smiled. "But they need to know that you have their back. Even more, they need to believe that you would step in front of them and protect them."

"How so?" Rae asked.

"Let's say one of your salespeople made a mistake. Big or small, it doesn't matter. But when you saw it, you immediately stepped in and took ownership of that mistake, helping them save face. Perhaps you failed to tell them something they needed to know—whatever the situation was, instead of letting them take the fall, you stepped in. And in doing so, you showed them that they can count on you, they can trust you, and you do truly care about them."

"I can see where this all fits together, especially right now during my mission to understand and know my team," said Rae. "It's kind of fascinating, Dan."

"It is, isn't it? It's also vital to every leader's success. By abiding by these laws, you can be assured that your team will accept, even seek, your leadership, and you'll know that the members of your team will respond to your leadership favorably. That's effective leadership, and it's what every leader should bring to their team."

"Wow, I can't believe how profound these laws are, but I can see how they anchor to all the lessons you've taught me. And I can see how applying them makes it easier to have effective hard conversations," Rae responded.

"Well, keep in mind that not everyone will love the direct and clear conversations you will need to have with them. But I believe that clear is kind, and most people will respect you for being willing to be honest with them, even if what you have to say may be hard for them to hear. But you're right, when they know that you care about them, that you trust them, and have confidence in them, the hard conversations don't feel as hard. The truth is, I've found these tough conversations to be the biggest reason I've lost sleep over the years. There have been times I've been up all night thinking about a tough conversation I needed to have. It's one of the reasons leaders revert to the tailboard."

"What does that mean—revert to the tailboard?"

"Reverting to the tailboard is something that can happen when leaders find themselves in an uncomfortable spot. A friend of mine, who's a firefighter shared it with me, and it pertains to firefighters who promote into leadership. For starters, do you know what a tailboard is?"

"No, I can't say that I do," she replied.

"The tailboard is the back step on the fire truck where they pull the hoses from. When someone promotes through the ranks and finds themselves in a situation they aren't comfortable with, they revert to the rank where they are the most comfortable. They revert to the tailboard. It's a thing with firemen and all types of leaders, actually. And it happens more than you know."

"The problem with reverting to the tailboard is that it means that the person is no longer doing the job that they're supposed to do, but rather duplicating effort, freelancing or being completely ineffective because they've neglected their leadership duty. They revert to the tailboard because they're not comfortable being a leader."

"Then what happens?" Rae asked.

"My friend told me the best way he's found to prevent 'reverting to the tailboard' is for leaders to create a strong foundation in the position they hold, proper delegation, solid leadership training and trusting in their team to be effective in pulling someone out of 'revering' in a stressful situation."

"Which is what you've been doing with me! You've been preparing me to be comfortable in my role by providing me with training and helping me build a strong foundation with your leadership principles and laws," Rae acknowledged.

"Well, I do want to prepare you—I won't always be here, and I want to provide you with the tools and fundamental principles to succeed, Rae. You see, people are not natural born leaders. Great leaders are made. It's a journey, a learning process, if you will. I call it 'Sell-er-ship.'" Dan smiled.

"Sell-er-ship ..." Rae mulled over the word. "I like that, Dan. Going from selling to leadership, captured in one word. That's the journey I'm on!"

"Glad you like it—now it's time for you to take ownership of it. Embrace the laws and principles and apply them generously with your team. One of the most rewarding parts of being a leader is watching your team members grow and blossom as you do. That's been the biggest reward in my leadership career, and I know it will be yours, too."

(10) The Mentee Becomes the Mentor

Nearly two years later, Rae had solidified herself as a great leader, something which Dan had reminded her was not easy for a successful salesperson to accomplish. It hadn't always been easy. In fact, there were times when it was downright tough. But over time, she became more confident in her role and, as a result, became an increasingly positive influence on her team. While she attributed her success to Dan's patience and principles, she also knew that her success was her responsibility. It was exactly what she told her sales teams, "I can give you the tools to succeed, but it is up to you to put them to use."

During the last couple years, she had watched Coral absolutely blossom in her role as a salesperson. As her people skills grew, so did her sales numbers. She had become an integral part of Rae's sales team, and the vibrant, yet caring, personality that had emerged made her one of the most-liked members of the team.

But it was Matt who Rae looked upon with the most pride. In her opinion, he had the most to overcome. Coral had to overcome someone else's criticism and judgement, but Matt had to conquer his own criticism and disapproval, which had been at times harsh.

Under Rae's guidance, though, he had made great strides. He learned to forgive himself for not living up to his own expectations and started to celebrate his successes. As a result, he enjoyed even more of them. After the first quarter of the last year, Rae was surprised to find that Matt was actually on target to become one of the top sales leaders in the division—a feat that wasn't easy, but one she applauded.

By the end of the year, Matt had accomplished another goal, and in true form, he gave Rae credit for making it happen.

"Rae, at one point, I didn't have a job. Then, I had a job, but I struggled with it. It was hard for me to accept the fact that things wouldn't always go my way. But with your help, I now know that sometimes that's okay. And I thank you for that. Not only did you give me this opportunity, but you showed me how to succeed at it. I have to tell you, I never thought I'd love sales, but I do. I couldn't imagine doing anything I love more," he'd said when she congratulated him for reaching a milestone.

Again, Rae was reminded of how much Matt reminded her of herself. She, too, had never believed that she'd love being a leader, but here she was, loving every minute of it so much that she found she implemented the principles she'd learned in every area of her life.

"In some ways, they're universal principles and laws, aren't they, Dan?" she observed.

"Oh, most certainly. They've been the foundation of my success, and I have to be honest, there was a time I had my own misgivings about my leadership abilities," he admitted.

"You? No way!" Rae countered.

"Oh, yes. I know it might be hard to believe, but there was a time when I was reluctant to become a leader. After all, I was doing good in sales, even great. It didn't make sense for me to throw that away to accept a leadership role, especially since initially it would mean a pay cut—something I really didn't want. Then my mentor pointed out to me the potential for a huge long-term upside if I was successful with my teams. Looking back, I've actually made a hundred times more than I would have from just selling. And that doesn't take into account the other benefits, which are perhaps even more valuable. Money cannot replace the fulfillment I've enjoyed throughout my career. I'll be forever grateful for that," he said.

"And there's more to come!" Rae exclaimed.

"Actually, Rae, that's something I want to talk to you about. I've been doing a great deal of thinking, and I think it's time for me to retire," he informed her.

"Retire? What?"

"I'm sorry to catch you off guard, but one of the benefits of success is that it gives you the ability to do some things you wouldn't otherwise be able to do," he said.

"Such as?" asked Rae.

"Rae, I've been asked to serve a mission for my church. It's something I've always said I would do if I was ever asked to do it. In fact, I've secretly always wanted to, but it's not something you can just appoint yourself to. You have to be called by the church leaders to go."

"Well, my wife and I got the call, and we're fortunate enough to be in a position to do it—so we're excited to go."

"What's this mission?" she asked. "Where are you going and when?"

"We will be relocating to Spokane, Washington for three years. It's a volunteer role, meaning it's unpaid, but the rewards can't be measured in any terms, including money. We'll be presiding over a couple hundred young volunteer missionaries, ranging in age from 18 to 25."

"I've accomplished what I set out to do here, Rae, and so, so much more. Now, I have the opportunity to impact a lot of other lives, including a group of young missionaries who I'm looking forward to teaching what I've taught you and others here at Champion—but this time, I can channel these teachings in more of a spiritual way."

"It sounds incredible, Dan. Truly it does, but are you sure you're ready for this and ready to retire? You still have so much to offer to the company, and to me," Rae pointed out.

"I'm sure. I'm fortunate enough to be in good health and in a position to retire without any financial worries. I would be doing myself, my church, and a bunch of young missionaries in Spokane a disservice if I didn't answer this call to serve. And you better believe I'll be giving out a lot of lollipops and lemonade!" Dan chuckled.

"That sounds impressive, and I can see how much it means to you. It shouldn't surprise me—after all, this is who you are. You've always gladly stepped up to help a person or a cause, and you've encouraged every member of this organization to do the same," Rae said. "I'm sure you'll do amazing on your mission, Dan! I just wish you didn't have to go."

"I'll be around for a while, Rae, until the beginning of June, but I report to Spokane the first week in July. I want to make sure there's a smooth transition here. Remember, I have a stake in this company and its success, as well as yours and everyone who works for us. Which brings me to the second thing I want to talk to you about," he said.

"What's that?"

"Rae, I'd like you to consider filling my shoes as division president," he smiled.

"What? Me? Are you kidding! I'm not ready for that!" she exclaimed.

"I beg to differ. You are ready. I've watched as you've become quite an impressive leader. This is the next logical step in your career, and I have every faith that you will be an asset to our company."

"While I appreciate your confidence, Dan, I'm just not so sure. I've always had you here to turn to when I needed advice, but there's no guarantee that I can be successful without you," she admitted.

"There are never any guarantees, but I do know that my job is to prepare my leaders to be successful without me. Remember when we talked about the days when we helped our kids learn how to ride a bike? Well, Rae, I've been walking alongside you, but if I continue to do that, you'll never know how far you can go on your own. A good leader knows when it's time to let go, and I think it's time. You're ready, Rae, and I'm sure you'll go far. In the meantime, we have a lot of work to do. I want the transition to be as seamless as possible, and I'm counting on you to make that happen."

***

The sendoff for Dan was fitting for a division president who had made such a significant impact on the lives and careers of so many people. In his honor, the company closed for the afternoon, and the doors were open for the employees and members of his church and community to celebrate this new chapter in his life.

When it was all over, Rae finally found an opportunity to thank her leader, her mentor, and friend and wish him well on his journey.

"I can't thank you enough for everything you've done for me, Dan. You've taught me everything I know."

"I don't like to think of it as an education, Rae. Instead, it's a journey—the journey of sellership that brought you to where you are today. And I want to thank you for being on that journey with me. I've truly enjoyed watching you grow, and I know great things are in store for you. I'd like to wish you luck as the new division president, but I think I'd prefer instead to wish you skuck!"

"Skuck! What's that?" Rae laughed.

"SKUCK is skill plus luck. Luck favors action. Get skucky! You've proven you have the skills to be a great salesperson and a great leader. You don't need luck, but you'll find it comes to you naturally. The more you do, the more you succeed, the luckier you'll get. I thank God every day for skuck. The more I've done something I love, whether personally or professionally, the better I've become and the luckier I've gotten. Now, Rae, I wish that for you. In fact, I have a feeling that things are going to continue to go your way," he said as he handed her his keys, officially transferring ownership of his role to her.

Before she could reply, Matt walked up to wish Dan well in his new adventure.

"It sounds exciting, sir! Make sure you keep us updated from time to time, I'm sure I speak for everyone here when I say we'd love to hear from you," he said, then apologized for interrupting their conversation before he walked away.

"It's been a pleasure to watch Matt grow, Rae. I'm sure he'll be an asset to you down the road," Dan remarked, flashing her one of his signature smiles.

Rae knew precisely what he was talking about. In fact, it was something she'd wanted to talk to Matt about all day.

"I'm sure he will," Rae agreed. "And if you'll excuse me for a minute, I'm going to catch him before he leaves."

"Matt! Matt!" she said as she picked up her pace to catch up to him.

Turning abruptly at the sound of his name, Matt stopped to let Rae catch up.

"I wanted to catch you before you leave," Rae said.

"Sure, Rae. What can I do for you?" Matt asked.

"Well, with Dan setting out on a new journey, I thought you might be interested in a journey of your own," Rae smiled.

"What kind of journey?"

"Let's just say it's a journey of sellership."

"Sellership? What's that?"

"Well, I'll tell you all about it," she replied as they walked toward the entry door of Champion's home office. "I can't promise it will be easy, but I can promise that it is one journey that will transform your life."

SCAN ME

Congratulations for finishing *Sellership*—you are among the elite who are finishers! We hope you have been able to get a lot of value from this book, and we thank you for placing your trust in us and reading it to the end. For additional FREE resources, scan this QR code to access training videos expounding on the principles of Sellership.

BEN WARD

Ben Ward is a passionate leader with over 20 years of experience in sales leadership and executive leadership training and development. Starting his career in direct sales as a door-to-door salesman, he quickly advanced to senior management in one of the fastest-growing companies in America.

At age 26, Ben built and managed the highest producing sales region at Firstline Security, an INC 500 company. He became the #1 highest producer in the company and generated over $37 million in revenue with sales teams. There he earned his first million dollars in sales commission. Ben went on to co-found Elevate Inc., an IP-based company which went public in 2010. He then became CEO/administrator of a Plum Healthcare facility, where he spent four years focused on leadership development and growing and developing a team of over 200 healthcare professionals.

In 2016, Ben took on the role of Executive Director of Leadership, Culture and Sales at LuLaRoe, where he helped more than 80,000 independent retailers and 2,300 internal employees with leadership development and sales growth. He participated in the generation of over $4 billion in sales within the company's first five years as an organization. Ben founded Forward Leadership as a result of his personal obsession for continuous improvement and passion for helping others grow and develop.

Ben specializes in Leadership Training and Development/ Culture, Productivity, and Sales & Recruiting. He is a keynote speaker, mentor, and strategic advisor.

On a personal note, Ben is a devoted husband and father, who has been playing ping-pong ever since he was in diapers and loves to play any chance he gets! (And might always keep a ping-pong paddle in the trunk of his car ;)

Learn more at www.forwardleadership.com

DR. GREG REID

For over 25 years, Greg has inspired millions of people to take personal responsibility to step into the potential of their greatness and, as such, his life of contribution has been recognized by government leaders, a foreign Princess, as well as luminaries in education, business, and industry.

Mr. Reid has been published in over 100 books, including 32 best-sellers in 45 languages. Titles, such as *Stickability: The Power of Perseverance; The Millionaire Mentor,* and *Three Feet from Gold: Turn Your Obstacles into Opportunities,* have inspired countless readers to understand that the most valuable lessons we learn are also the easiest ones to apply.

Greg Reid is known best for being Founder of Secret Knock, a Forbes and Inc. magazine top-rated event focused on partnership, networking, and business development. He is the producer of the Oscar-qualified film, *Wish Man,* based on the creator of the Make A Wish Foundation, streaming on Netflix now.

For his work in mentoring youth in his hometown of San Diego, Mr.

Reid was honored by the White House, where a former President commended Greg for positively working with youth through a local mentorship program. And if that is not enough, Greg was recently honored with a star in the infamous Las Vegas Walk of Stars.

www.GregReid.com

Made in the USA
Middletown, DE
21 February 2022

61491016R00076